A Pet Sitter's Day

By

Diana Carter

Introduction

When I started writing this book, it was a whole lot shorter. Twenty years ago, I thought that if I just wrote a magazine article explaining what a pet sitter does in the course of a day, I wouldn't have to keep explaining it to potential clients and curious strangers. I found out that selling an article to a magazine had magical hurdles that I did not know how to clear; furthermore, I lost interest in it because business was very good and I had plenty to do. I had to come to love my work, and actually enjoyed talking about it to anyone who would listen.

The idea stayed with me, and after a few years, I realized I knew a bit more than the average person about pet care. A person in my position has the benefit of a breadth of experience as well as the collective knowledge of clients. Asking good questions of vets and groomers adds even more to the knowledge base. The same year that I started the business I had adopted Maggie, a Labrador retriever puppy, and she became my steady companion. As time went by I knew that eventually I would tell our story. I kept the original notes, expanding them and finally writing an outline for a book.

Now I've done it. My life as a pet sitter is here, along with some of the best memories of my life with Maggie. My hope is that pet lovers will better understand what pet sitters do, for people still ask me about it, whether or not they utilize the service. I would certainly be pleased if the pet sitting industry, which has been so good for me, were to benefit from what I've written.

Of course, conversations have been reconstructed. My original notes were from a day in September of 1993. Material was subsequently lost and added over time. I consciously altered the phone calls to demonstrate an informative range of calls I'm likely to get in a day. Because the janitorial aspect of the work is a given, I edited out some of that as well.

As for my sweet, abiding friend, Maggie always did everything better and faster than I did. She lived her life in full in just a little over sixteen years. It was a good life. She was, after all, a pet sitter's dog. She rode in the car nearly every day and knew well our public parks and city squares. Maggie's friends included humans, dogs, cats and horses. Ever the teacher, she eventually helped me learn about the needs of aging pets.

I make my rounds alone now, but I remain a student, with my heart and mind open to new possibilities.

CHAPTER 1

5:30 Feet on the Floor

Okay, okay, I'm awake. Why does 5:30 come so soon? Oh, and once I stir, however slightly, or open my eyes, I will have made the commitment to Get Up and Feed the Pets (can they hear my eyelids click?). Oh, I'm not complaining. This is truly one fine life, and I'm going to share just one day of it with you. After getting myself ready for the day and feeding my pets, we'll be on the road, taking care of other people's spoiled animals. I can't make you envy me, but I don't know why you wouldn't. Here goes.

"Hello, sweet Katherine." As long as Katherine Katz is standing on my chest, we're going nowhere. This is one pretty girl and she knows it. This black and white tabby with a white face and white feet has a mesmerizing way of gazing at me with those large, dark eyes, something she's done since the day she first opened them. She knows she'll get what she wants, but her challenge is to use telepathy on a human with apparently faulty brain waves. "Of course, I'll pet you first." How I love that purr. Deep and smooth, downright sultry. Surprising volume, too, for a five-pound kitty. Where does it all come from? I've always thought that I should record this amazing sound. After sixteen years, the chances of that are slim. I'm just like everyone else – sometimes too busy to do the really important stuff. So this marvelous sound remains my special pleasure, and – one day- just a happy memory.

"What can I do with such a cat as you? Yes, I'll scratch your chin. Oh, look at that little heart-shaped face. No wonder my boy-cats have all loved you so. What a loving sweetheart. Okay, I'm coming to my senses. This is really just about breakfast, no? Come on – move over, so I can crawl out of here." Of course, no matter how gingerly I relocate her, Katherine always gives me a long, indignant stare, then jumps down and leaves the room. If she had her way, all events would be her idea. Cuddling would take up most of her schedule. Look at that. She's even beautiful walking away. She has a white bottom with a black hourglass centered perfectly under her tail.

"Well, good morning, Maggie." My precious chocolate Lab, and the main attraction around here. "Come here and gimme kiss. Hey! Get off of me! Yes, we're going to get up, but not if you're standing on my chest. Why is this everybody's favorite place to stand? Oh, yes, you're a sweetheart, too. Yes, you are. That's right, flop over." This is our chance for quality time before the day carries us off. "Back rub? No? Tummy rub, then." Ah, yes. Always a favorite. Even her breathing changes. Maggie's like any other dog – I could do this until her fur wore off and it wouldn't be too much.

"Now where's my kiss? Oh, sure, jump down. Go chase the cats down the steps." I guess she caught a glimpse of little Silky Black, so the race is on. My next chance for one of her stingy kisses will be tomorrow morning. That's her rule, and I understand it about as well as she probably understands some of my rules. At this stage in our friendship, we accept each other's ways without question.

And there she goes, bumping down the stairs. She isn't running, but rather sliding, sitting almost like a person on a playground slide. Heaven knows we've done that enough times. I don't have to see it — I've seen the chase countless times — bearing down on that left hip, as if she thought that made her go faster, and her ear flaps blown back. She'll somehow manage to hit the living room floor on all four feet, and careen sharply to the left into the living room, missing the front door by inches. As she scrambles through the room, Silky Black has surely already streaked through the dining room, through the cat door and down the cellar steps to safety.

Maggie's mornings would be incomplete if she didn't chase Silky Black through the house. Silky is a shiny black cat, a lightning-fast five-pounder, and Maggie has never come close to catching her. When Maggie was a puppy it was a pursuit in earnest for her. It took her a long time to realize what Silky has always known, that's it's merely an amusing exercise that always ends the same way.

Well, we can talk later. This is where I may very well be different from you. Right now, as my feet touch the floor, I know that only I care what kind of day I have. Self-employment. A fantasy many people harbor. Free to follow my dreams, and free to starve to death. Not to worry — I plan my days well in advance, and starvation is not on the schedule. Okay, here we go. Shower, a little make-up, and a minor miracle for the hair, then a day of running around Lorain County. Okay, wait – let's consider the weather. Sun, wind, a little rain later. Hey, it's the Great Lakes region. So, no make-up and no hairdo. Waste of time. Quick shower – don't run away. Oh, and I'll clean out the cat pans while I'm in there, too.

****

Now, what to wear – this should be the easy part, but it's where I have to wake up fully and recall what and who are on the schedule. Dressing for the office was easy. A suit's a suit, and that indoor climate was wonderfully controlled. Dressing for field social work was trickier, and in some ways a good background for what I do now. The roster was different every day and weather was a factor, too. I had to know if I was going to see a wealthy client who was also a financial contributor to the agency's causes. Sometimes I was going into a neighborhood where I might have to make a dash for the car. Then there were the sweet old ladies who had "ankle nippers," those little dogs that would latch onto my pant legs as I was leaving. That was my first inkling as a life-long animal lover that there were some animals in this world that I might not find appealing. Well, anyway, back to the ones I'll be caring for today. So, the weather, where I'm going and who I'm going to see. A couple of layers, I'm thinking. Short sleeves, because I've got that adorable sleeve-eating Golden retriever midday. No, I'll take a long-sleeve shirt – one she's already chewed – in case it gets cooler when that rain rolls in. Wet September days can be raw. Jeans, always jeans. Durable, not likely to pick up much hair, and so protective against pet claws. Let me try to remember the schedule– bird, cat, poodle, Dobermans, Bichon, the Golden. And I think I have those horses today. Let me grab a cap to hide my hair and we'll run downstairs.

Okay, wait. Just one more minute. You may have seen an image of a pet sitter that shows up in TV commercials from time to time – a petite twenty-something woman in tight jeans or shorts, sparkling white sneakers and ankle socks, snug tank top and a perky blond ponytail. She jogs delicately through a pristine park on a sunny day, with a well-behaved poodle or Shih Tzu on the end of a leash. She is smiling. Her posture is perfect. She will never break a sweat. She will never step in anything that must be scraped off later.

What do I know? Maybe that's what they look like in the big city. A very different notion that seems to prevail in market areas like mine is that pet sitters are people who just can't get real jobs. For me, too many conversations with old acquaintances have run aground when I've mentioned what I do for a living. Those faces suddenly drawn long with pity used to make me feel as if I had to explain myself. Now they make me laugh. And you - well, unless you're a pet sitter or know one, you may not know what to think either. Here it is in a nutshell. I run a business that I created out of thin air at my dining room table. I earn a steady income, own my own home, and can buy whatever I want in the grocery store. These are the best days of my life, and yes, I'm amazed that I have the wisdom to recognize that.

Okay, now this is fun. I walk by this full- length mirror in the hallway every morning and I like what I see. I'm not the perky blond gal in the park, just an aerobically fit middle-aged woman in a T-shirt and jeans, auburn hair stuffed under an olive green ball cap. Not bad, in my opinion, and I have plenty of opinions, by the way. You know, I stopped in front of this mirror every morning for years, checking my lipstick, fussing with my hair, or straightening a scarf. Never really saw myself, never really knew myself. I just dashed off to jobs that sometimes felt like sentences to be served. These days are different. I check myself out and break into a crazy grin. I know who I am, I know what I'm doing and I'm glad to be in the world. How did I get so lucky? Well, I found my "luck" at the bottom of a very dark hole, and that may or may not be a topic for later. Let's take Maggie outside, and then we'll feed the kitty crew.

"Hey! You came back up! Maggie, show me how good you are." This is where she used to race me down the steps and try to push me out of the way. Foolish of me that I didn't train her better, and sooner. She's my first and only dog, and I've made many of the same mistakes other first-timers do. Watch this. "Maggie, stay." As I go down the stairs, she sits on the landing until I release her with "okay." We just need to be out of her way when she gets that release word. She may not be built for speed, but she doesn't know it. Here we go.

"Okay." What a racket. I've considered carpeting the steps, but for now there's something wonderful about that thunderous galumphing. "Good girl. What's your hurry? I know - breakfast."

Yes, waiting at the top of the steps is a practice dogs can easily learn, but I wonder how many dog owners teach it. As a pet sitter, I don't see a lot of training going on. Many people do as I used to do – they learn to put up with "inconvenient" behavior. I'm always on the lookout for good books on dog obedience, and now Maggie is in school all the time. I believe all dogs should be in training – yep, all the time. Well, maybe not every moment, but she is my guinea pig. When I find a promising book on training, I bring it home and try the program on my own sweetie. We have both benefitted from every book so far. I enjoy the challenge of trying to be smarter than my dog and being the one in charge, and Maggie seems to enjoy playing along.

So training Maggie not to be underfoot is one thing, but now we come to the kitchen, where we have a sea of hungry cats. Katherine Katz, Sam Gold, Herbie, Shadow, and Silky Black are masters at that crazy milling around that spoiled cats do when they want to convince their humans that they're starving.

"Yes, good morning, everyone. Let me pick up Sammy. Hey, bud, I just love you. My sweet golden boy. Where did you sleep last night? You weren't in the bedroom this morning. Not telling? Okay, stop wiggling. Down you go." He and my all-black Shadow are my two long-hairs.

Phone messages? Nope. In this business, it's possible to get calls at all hours, so I'm always checking. Clients call to say they got in early, or that they've been delayed. Some will call because I've asked them to confirm their return when they have high-maintenance pets. My phones are always muted. I'd never get any sleep otherwise.

Before we can get Maggie out the door, we must first locate Herbie. He's the mouthy little tabby with the white face and the Bette Davis eyes. He's usually lurking near the door. He is low to the ground and lightning fast. We can't let him get out. The last time he got out, he was gone for two days. He showed up filthy and exhausted, and missing his collar. Herbie has escaped several times and I've taught myself not to worry about him. I used to feel as though I had lost track of a child, and my insides were in knots with fear. Of course, Herbie is an adult. My human vanity tells me he has everything he needs in the house, but that's wrong thinking, too. He can't hunt or have creepy adventures in the house. And Herbie is one competent cat. What would I myself want to do with excellent night vision, retractable claws,fangs, keen hearing, and the ability to climb trees and leap five times my height? And if I were just like Herbie, add rapid reflexes and cunning to the list of attributes. Hunting, anyone?

"Hey, Herbie! Good morning, sweetheart. You look sleepy." It could be a fake-out. Yes, he's just that smart. Maggie goes out the door first, then I'll follow, walking backwards. I know- walking backwards is a foolish thing to do under any circumstances, but we are dealing with Herbie. He and every other animal I know have reduced me to foolishness at some time or other.

"C'mon, Mag, let's go out." She practically flies down those steps to the patio. She's known her boundaries for years, and as long as I'm outside with her, she'll stay close. We don't need a fence. She's a great Lab, no prey drive whatsoever. Chases bunnies and birds, with no real interest in catching them. She just runs up to them, then stops. She's never barked, either. "That's a good girl." She makes a dash for the evergreens in the far northeast corner of the back yard. They're her privacy screen. She's such a lady at times. We can wander back in that direction and I'll show you the herb garden.

The Sweet Annie is almost six feet tall this year. I'll wait until it dries a bit more and hang it on my dining room wall. Wild animals eat the tamer stuff, like parsley, and the stray cats destroy the catnip. I'm left with the more pungent plants, so I have enough chives, oregano and sage to give away.

I've always had an herb garden, and with some magical expansion of hours in the day, I plan to learn about the benefits of herbs for pets. Someday.

"Hey! Maggie, you sneak!" As soon as I'm not thinking about her, she comes from behind and clips me at full gallop. She always manages to barely graze me - otherwise she'd knock me down. Some mornings we chase each other for a while. With any luck, the neighbors will see us and think I'm crazy. You have nothing to worry about. She's very polite to strangers. Well, unless you're a male, in which case she'll want to worship you. And no, I can't explain that. I can guess that since she sees so few men, she thinks they are gods or space aliens.

"Well, look who's here for breakfast. Where have you been, Kiki?" This is her habit, if you can call it that. Kiki Leekee is the sweetest calico. Her wide baby face does not match her reputation as the neighborhood tramp. I'm hoping to catch her one day and have her spayed. In the meantime, I feed her, help her with her deliveries, and keep or adopt out her offspring. Kiki generally shows up every two or three days for a meal, until she gets pregnant. Then she disappears to who-knows-where until she's ready to deliver. But, oh, she comes back. She seems to know where she's safe. Heaven knows I don't need any more cats, but I won't let them go, either. Their life outside would likely be unhappy and short. Would you like another cat? No,of course not. Everyone has as many as they can handle. That's the state of things today. Multiple- cat households, and rescue programs and humane societies teeming with strays. More communities are organizing trap and release programs for feral cats. That kind of management only makes sense. Some of the barbarians in public office continue to push for mass euthanasia of strays and ferals. Ha! It's not only inhumane. It reveals a serious lack of understanding of the problem. We don't have a few pests yowling in alleyways. We have millions of homeless cats. It's a huge problem, and both the cause and the solution sit at the feet of humankind. We need to let the animals teach us a few things, instead of just reacting to the problems we think they have created.

I'm just about out of friends who'll take Kiki's kittens, so I'm more eager than ever to spay this little mother. Any ideas on how to catch her? I can't think of any creature more wily than an intact female cat. They are in cahoots with Mother Nature to reproduce as much as possible. Astounding, since feline reproduction is evidently no fun, and females are capable of being pregnant most of the time. The active males are just as miserable, going from one fight to the next. Dreadful. We need to become smarter than they are and to take responsibility for them, but what are the chances?

"Come on, Maggie. You, too, Kiki. Let's get some breakfast." Don't let Herbie out. See? He's hovering, always hopeful, hunkered down between these antique crocks lined up against the wall. "Herbie, you are not invisible. Scoot!"

"Oh, Maggie, someday you're going to be perfect." She puts herself in a sit-stay in the kitchen doorway while I feed the cats. They get the good stuff, so I have to measure. "Okay, guys and gals, no pushing. And don't trip me." They still expect a little dry food, but they eat mostly raw ground turkey with pumpkin puree and a side of plain yogurt.

Kiki came in, so Cujo can't be far behind. He's the world's sweetest boy cat, just recently retired from tom-catting. We'll listen for him – he sounds pathetic when he thinks he'll miss breakfast. So, Herbie, Silky Black, Katherine Katz, Sam Gold, and Shadow each get a bowl. Kiki and Cujo will share. Wait - there he is now. I'll never understand how every cat can make his own "meow" distinctive, but it is the case.

"Hey, sweet boy, come on in. Did you sleep in the barn last night?" The very handsome and muscular tabby Cujo was Kiki's lover before The Big Ride, and he still guards his territory. I'm hoping he'll keep the toms away until I can trap Kiki. He's done a good job for almost a year, and I know my luck is running out.

See how they run from bowl to bowl? Everyone gets the same thing, and they should know that by now. It looks so familiar. They think that what everybody else has must be better. It's one of the few things cats do that remind me of classic human behavior.

"And, Maggie, the highlight of your morning is coming right up." I still feed her kibble, although I'm ambivalent about it. I break an egg over it – with the shell! You don't know what a kick that is until you do it. My perfectionist mother would gasp to see anyone leave so much as a tiny fragment of shell behind. Honestly, it's a great rush. The real payoff is watching Maggie curl back her lips while she crunches it. She also gets unsweetened applesauce with cinnamon, flax oil, and some boiled chicken. We'll go full-out raw someday, when I feel more confident about what I'm doing. Everything is a work in progress around here, including me.

Now it's my turn, time for some hot coffee and a piece of black raspberry pie. Life is good, but it's so much better with homemade pie. I stand at the kitchen sink and eat. A big eat-in kitchen and a formal dining room notwithstanding, the best place to eat is right here, at this section of kitchen counter that passes for office space. I have my phone, appointment book, rolodex, and a calendar all in one place.

More often than not, when I answer the phone, I'm chewing on something. Speaking of that, I just love the seeds in berries. Always did. I love food with a lot of texture. This is truly good pie. The berries are from those wild shoots that the birds must have planted in the back yard. I allow the canes to mature just enough to produce a good crop of berries. By that I mean enough berries to fill a pie shell. Then they have to go. Next year, I'll suffer the beastly things to bring berries somewhere else in the yard. Some aspect of the yard is always a bit wild. I'd be truly crazy in a controlled suburban setting. Well, I'll take the coffee with me. I have learned to enjoy coffee at any temperature. I never re-heat it – it becomes a different product when you do that. Yuck!

There's nothing in voice mail, so that means no last-minute bookings or cancellations, no one came home early from a trip, and no perverts with my phone number had insomnia last night.

I'm always trying to feed my pets better. One day it occurred to me that if I ate just some kind of dry cereal and drank fresh water every day of my life, I would survive. But would it be enough? Well, of course not. Shoot, I'm an omnivore. And these sweet darlings? Well, they're carnivores. Or at least the cats are. Maggie's tribe is made of hunters and scavengers, but thanks to all those millennia hanging around humans, they are also omnivores. So, why have we been happy just throwing down kibble in front of our pets for so long? We should be grateful our animal friends don't complain. They might have let us know a long time ago that this was never enough. Dry food is just convenience food at best, junk food at worst.

When I was growing up, many dogs and cats ran free, and there was still plenty of habitat. Our pets were always dragging home fresh kill. The kibble my mother set out for the pets provided back-up for when the hunting didn't go well. That practice seemed to work just fine until people began to keep their pets indoors. Cats are obligate carnivores, so the food that's best for them over the long term is meat, preferably raw. My vet once said that it's too bad we can't put live mice in cans. Dogs do better with a varied diet because they're more adaptable. Well, let's face it – they're scavengers. They can eat anything. In any case, they still need high quality food in the long term.

So many people are just now becoming conscious of what's in pet food, and I see it as a pet sitter. Some of my clients still give their dogs kibble, but add shredded cheese, yogurt, or bits of meat. When I've asked them why they do it, they usually express some vague idea that dry food out of a bag surely can't be enough. That's what I say. Let the label reading begin.

"Kiki, out you go, before we have a situation." She never uses a litter pan, and I have actually seen her try to keep her kittens out of them, too. Her last kitten was Shadow. He was an "only" kitten, and Kiki had spent little time with him, behaving almost as if one kitten wasn't worth her best maternal effort. I was stopped in my tracks the day I saw her nudging him away from the small cat pan I had set up for him in the corner of the kitchen. He was just a little ball of black fur then, and he wasn't sure whether she or I was his mother. He chose to take her advice just then when she made odd, yowling vocalizations while scratching the floor. He squatted on the floor and peed, while Kiki purred approvingly. You don't have to believe me, because I wouldn't believe it if I hadn't seen it myself. Cat mothers are authoritative teachers. And if you're wondering, I still have to "re-direct" Shadow from time to time.

"Okay, Kiki, be good. Stay out of the street." Yes, I talk to them as if they understand English. Kiki is likely to walk in the street with no apparent fear. Cujo has never, to my knowledge, gone anywhere near the street. Those two have always been outdoor cats, and my long-term goal is to get them indoors for good. Not always an easy conversion to make, but worth the effort.

Let me double-check my tote bag – pouch full of tagged house keys, binder with copies of service agreements, water bottle, billfold, notebook, biz cards, Maggie's leash, and the umbrella. And, in my pocket and in the tote, the sign of a true pro, wads of plastic bags. Change of clothing, extra leashes, enzyme cleaner, paper towels and a box of latex gloves are always in the trunk.

"C'mon, Mag. The day is brightening. Let's go uncover Popcorn's cage. I'll bring you back before the day gets too warm." Maggie always jumps in the back, and starts out facing forward like a person. Before you know it, she'll be stretched out and sound asleep.

It's a short trip across town. It isn't quite 7:00, so the college students won't be on the street yet. They're darters, you know. They walk right out in front of moving cars all the time. Some drivers slam on their brakes for them, but I strongly believe that the leaders of tomorrow should learn to follow traffic laws.

Speaking of creatures that play chicken with cars, let me say something about Kiki Leekee. I have a soft spot in my heart for her, so I can't let you think she has been nothing but a lousy mother. She was, in one incident I witnessed, a spectacularly protective parent.

One warm August evening, from the screened porch came sounds of a snarl-snap-growl commotion complete with the violent moving about of the cats' food bowls. Kiki and Cujo ate out there in those days, and Shadow was a tiny kitten, living there in a wooden crate. Kiki's only other kitten in that litter had been an orange tiger, but he lived just briefly. Anyway, that night about six large and very hungry raccoons had broken through the screen, searching for food. They were followed by more raccoons, and I could hardly get my breath as I counted to seventeen and stopped counting. I closed and locked the door. The scene was like something from one of those cheesy "imbalance of nature" flicks. I wanted so much to intervene, but I feared for my own safety.

Suddenly the noise level increased, with a layer of high-pitched yowling and hissing. The cats! Kiki and Cujo had just come home for the night, and found their sleeping kitten's box surrounded by a sea of hungry raccoons. I opened the door, prepared (foolishly) to fly into the middle of it all and chase the raccoons away. No need. All the raccoons but one were now fleeing through the torn screen and beyond the glow of the porchlight. An enraged Cujo cornered the straggler, an animal too scared to turn and run. Cujo stood up on his back legs, and used both paws – claws fully extended – to slash at him repeatedly. Kiki paced wildly behind Cujo, dividing her attention between the confrontation and the safety of her kitten. Long after that last raccoon had escaped, she continued to pace, growl, and spit. Her fur stood up along her spine, and her tail looked like a bottle brush.

Kiki showed herself to be a caring mother after all, and Cujo showed that he knew nothing of those stereotypes about "love 'em and leave 'em" tom cats. He is one fine daddy.

What a pretty morning! The sun is coming on strong through these big, beautiful trees. We're just like everywhere else – we don't have as many big trees as we used to, but they are still plentiful enough to feel like a lush gift. If that rain comes in later, there'll be no point in trying to walk any dogs today. Modern dogs do not like bad weather, including rain, snow and wind.

Here we go, off to see one very spoiled parakeet. I take care of very few birds, and they are usually part of multi-pet households. Popcorn is an "only pet." He gets uncovered with the sunrise, but goes to bed after sunset. A little strange, since most birds, in my experience, are on a schedule of either natural or artificial light, not a combination. Poppy is something of a night owl, but always wants to share breakfast with his owner, a college professor with morning classes.

"Maggie, you're already snoring."

We're passing Tappan Square on our left. On warm days, all those trees seem to cool the air by about ten degrees. When I first moved to this little town, I used to walk through the square at night, and the density of the trees made it too dark to see much of anything. Once, when I must have taken too long or smelled like dinner, a pack of wild dogs came running up to me in the darkness, biting at my hands. Very scary. Then we had the sad but adorable lone canine characters like Arithmetic Dog. He was a beagle mix with three legs, and spent his days begging food from people coming out of Gibson's Bakery or the Campus Restaurant. The surly packs and the scruffy loners are gone now, but so are many of those magnificent trees.

CHAPTER 2

7:00am A Ten-Dollar Bird

This is perfect. Just 7:00 now, and we'll go in quietly so we don't startle our little man-bird. I'll just call his name softly, which is what I always do with animals that are home alone. I love this old house with the high ceilings and the big window seat here in the living room. Like so many such houses, it has been chopped up into apartments. This apartment takes up most of the first floor, so the layout makes sense. We'll find Popcorn over here in a darkened room on the left.

"Hey, Poppy. Are you awake?" There- he's chirping softly. I always sing back, "Pop-pop-pop-pop-poppy, Poppy Popcorn." Somehow it seems reasonable to me that one day he's going to sing that nonsense back to me, but so far it only serves to silence him. Is he listening carefully? Does he like it? Would he sing it if he could? Does the sound intimidate him somehow? Why the silence? After all, he can whistle the theme to the old "Andy Griffith Show." And what's wrong with me? Why do I think this little creature could possibly care about anything right now but sunlight and food?

Here's his cage, in this room that also serves as his human's bedroom. We'll open the drapes to lighten the room a bit. He's always covered just so. His human showed me a particular way these sheets and blankets have to be placed for both coverage and air flow. We'll take them off, fold them, and put them away for tonight when we'll reverse the process. It's always been easy for me to remember animals' routines and where everything is kept for them. Nothing else in life stays in my mind that way.

"There's my sleepy boy. Let's open your cage. You look well." I always remove the layers of covering slowly and talk quietly. I have no idea how much time a parakeet needs to wake up and face the day. "Okay, jump onto my finger. Let's go build you a good breakfast." Poppy always steps onto my finger-perch deftly and without hesitation. I am humbled when I feel this tiny animal's complete trust in me as he readily clamps onto my finger and rides it into the kitchen. One detail that his human was very clear about was how to get him onto my finger. "Don't reach into the cage," she said. "Let him come to the door." Oh, I understood immediately – it's his room, his space.

"So, what'll it be? Always a little lettuce and a dab of yogurt. Wanna taste it? Here – let's put some yogurt on your plate, okay? Corn flakes? Sure. What does your human have in the produce bin – let's see. Blueberry? Why are you looking out the window? Was that a 'no' vote? What about apple? Ha! I thought so. Let's put a couple of small pieces out, on two different plates, cored and peeled. What do you have against blueberries?" This breakfast is more wholesome than mine.

I'm putting out two different seed mixes. I can't tell you what's different about them, and I bet Poppy's human isn't sure either. "Pop-pop-pop-pop-poppy." I've been making that silly sound for a long time now, and he has never picked it up. Don't ask me why it's a goal.

Okay, here's what I think I know about feeding birds. I'll rant about this while I clean up the kitchen. People with caged birds start out by buying some kind of seed or pellet mix, after which they start talking to more experienced people with birds. With more information, they incorporate other foods, such as nuts and fruit, based on what they pick up conversationally. The birds vote on their favorites, causing bird people to "edit" their food offerings. Poppy's human is different from any other bird steward I've worked for in that she takes him regularly to an avian veterinarian, and she's quite educated as to his needs. Guess what? Poppy's diet looks like the ones based on commercial availability and anecdote, although he also eats rice and pasta, broccoli, and cooked eggs. Everyone seems to come to the same understanding eventually via different roads.

A couple of years ago, I went to a series of meetings of a local organization of caged-bird lovers. Learning a thing or two about misting, bathing, beak and nail trimming made the meetings a good investment of my time. As it happens, I use none of my knowledge with Poppy.

"Okay, Popcorn, enjoy. I'm going to set up your playground." Back to the bedroom for this next step. Here's a pile of toys we have to set up across the bed, just like Poppy's own amusement park. I don't know how old some of these toys are, but I haven't seen some of this stuff anywhere for sale in years. He has three plastic, multi-colored Ferris wheels, umpteen pop-up penguins, miniature baby rattles – don't ask- and balls with bells in them that could be cat toys. We have a couple of plastic ladders. Let's just lean those up against this plastic cart, in case he decides to do some showing off. He seems to avoid the swings, but sometimes he lets me pull him around in one of the little wagons. Just for the record, I have never seen Poppy bother with much of anything here. His favorite activities remind me of my aging mother – he likes eating, napping and spying on the neighbors.

The members of the organization I mentioned earlier often said of themselves that they were all collectors, by their own characterization, of caged birds. No one had just one. Most had many birds. I like to think that they had ways of providing stimulating lives for their birds, but I suspect that most of those birds didn't live like Popcorn. He is truly one spoiled sweetheart.

Poppy can talk. His repertoire is limited, but it's cute. He stands on the little glass shelf in front of the medicine cabinet, blinks at himself in the mirror, and gives out a wolf whistle. Then he says, "Ooh, pretty bird." After a little strutting, he chortles, " I'm from Jersey."

Poppy presents a marvelous example of the way that animals are often inadvertently trained. As well as the best mimic, Poppy has captured the different registers and rhythms of English. When his human was working on her dissertation, she took up smoking. During the long hours she worked in the den on the computer and on the phone, she kept the door closed to protect Poppy from the smoke. He learned to chatter in a way that sounds like a conversation taking place in another room. The first time I heard this, I could swear I was hearing human speech through the wall. When I walked into the room where Poppy was perched, I realized the sound was coming out of his throat.

Poppy's human is involved with the New York theater scene, directing productions of Tennessee Williams's plays in apparently very small venues. One Sunday morning several months ago I was taking care of this little guy. When I uncovered him, I knew Poppy was sick. His droppings on the cage floor were liquid. He was bleary-eyed and his feathers were fluffed up, as if he felt an arctic chill.

I called the emergency number for his vet's practice, and was told that the avian vet who treated Poppy would be in church all day. They would try to reach him by cell phone, and if they could, he would probably call me within twenty minutes. The only number I had for Poppy's human was the theater. No one would be there that early.

I busied myself quietly cleaning out the bottom of the cage, and wiping down everything I could without disturbing Poppy. I changed his water. I put his covers back on, leaving about a 90 degree opening.

While I was watering plants, the vet called. Such a nice man, and he remembered Poppy. Clearly, calling from church, he had no records in front of him. Nonetheless, he had some recollection of when he had seen him last, and said that Poppy had had a similar episode about a year ago. He said that for now I should give him Pedialyte by dropper every two hours to rehydrate him, and that I should replace his water with it as well. I began to calculate the required changes in my schedule, but so what? I would do anything for Poppy Popcorn.

I have long known that animals still have at least one toe in the natural world. My own pets, especially the cats, taught me that they hide symptoms of illness or injury until they no longer can. In the wild, any indication of weakness would be asking for trouble. When I was younger, I used to wonder why I seemed not to notice that my pets were sick until their situations were dire. I thought I was just too self-absorbed to notice. I've since learned to read those subtle clues. The avian vet told me in that phone call that it isn't unusual for birds to show no symptoms, and then just suddenly reel off the perch and hit the floor of the cage, dead. Small birds are so vulnerable, they can't afford to let anyone know they're sick or injured. The vet seemed to think that since Poppy had the strength to sit on his perch and look uncomfortable, he had a good chance of pulling through.

I followed instructions to the letter. The vet had said I could give Gator Ade if I couldn't find Pedialyte. At the store, the power of marketing made me opt for the product sold for dehydrated babies, and not for the one sold as a "sports drink." Per the vet's instructions, I filled Poppy's water containers with Pedialyte, so it was all the liquid he had even when I wasn't there. Around 11:00 - again per vet's instructions - after his second swig of the stuff, Poppy was noticeably more comfortable. I then called the theater where I hoped to find his human in rehearsal. A young man answered, and when I asked to speak with Linda, he declared she was unavailable. I said, "Please tell her that her pet sitter called about her bird." I barely finished the sentence when the young man said, "Her pet sitter? Oh my God, please hold on." Poppy's human was very shortly on the phone, sounding breathless.

I assured her that Poppy seemed to be on the mend, and I was in contact with his vet. I would continue with the hydration regimen, and try giving him a little food. She said she wasn't worried, and I appreciated the lie. Of course she was worried, but I knew what she meant. She knew I would do all that was possible for him, as any real pet sitter would.

All this had a happy ending, with Poppy recovering within a day or so. I still smile when I think that this little blue bird could cause the interruption of a play rehearsal way off in New York City. Such is love.

Today Poppy is well, and that's what I prefer. Finding someone else's pet in need of care is far worse than if he were my own. Let me change the cage liner and wipe down the inside of the cage, and then we'll commune with the "sweet beast," as his human calls him.

She's got a cleaner in this spray bottle, and I don't know what it is. No fragrance, but I don't think it's water. Maybe an enzyme cleaner of some kind. I like being knowledgeable, but sometimes I give it a rest and just follow instructions. I figure all will be revealed eventually, and my clients are exceptional pet people. Even the stack of newspaper sections is handy. That woman is organized.

When there's a pet accident on any level of the house, it makes sense to have cleaning supplies handy. My house is set up that way, with cleaning rags and enzyme cleaner on every floor. Maggie's bath supplies are near the tub, and her leash hangs on a hook on the kitchen door. I'm always surprised at households where pet supplies are stashed in the basement or garage, or to be found no place in particular. I'm old enough to understand dealing with our pets' accessories as an afterthought – that's the way our parents did it. There was once more ambiguity about the place of pets in our lives. Since our pets are so much more a part of our families now, it makes sense for their belongings to be integrated into ours and kept handy.

Let's check the dining room. "Hey, Poppy. I thought you'd be here. Come on up. Let's nuzzle. Yes, you're such a sweet bird. Your mummie calls you a 'sweet beast.' I love you like crazy. Do you know you're the only bird I've ever known that I can cuddle with? Oh, yes, you are a chortling fool. I'm going now, so you can watch the neighborhood uninterrupted. Get some breakfast, young man. I'll be back later. I love you."

Here we go. I seldom see Poppy eat anything, but the food disappears. Wait, let me turn on the radio softly. The classical music of centuries past is Poppy's white noise. And we're out, making sure we can see Poppy as we secure the door.

We'll scoot over to Kendal now, so we can see the great Miss Kitty. This day has turned out to be lovely, warming up with actual sunshine that won't last for long. People in the know say about a third of our days in the Cleveland area are sunny, but it seems like less.

I never picked up any clients from the bird club, but a bird shop owner in Amherst has been a great source of business. When I started out, I visited every pet-related business in the area. Meeting Mary was like no other experience I've had so far. She was working with a couple of customers the first day I walked in, so I busied myself checking out the inventory and the set-up. She sold all manner of accessories and food for birds, and "boarded" a few birds in a back corner of the shop.

Mary was pleased to know about my business and immediately saw how she could help both of us. She said, "When people come in to board birds, but also have cats or dogs at home, I don't know what to tell them. I'll know now. They should let you take care of the entire crew. Besides, I'm not crazy about people hauling birds around. They're happier at home." A new marketing angle was born and a new ally was made.

Before I knew I was going to say it, I asked, "If I volunteer in your shop for a week, will you teach me about birds? I mean, I'm sure it takes more than a week to be knowledgeable, but I'd like to know how to handle them. I want to learn the fundamentals."

Mary smiled. "You don't need to work in my store. Got five minutes? I'll tell you everything you need to know for now."

"Seriously?"

"Just listen to me. Don't let birds get cold. Give them fresh water every day and feed exactly as their owners instruct. Every bird owner has a slightly different idea about what good nutrition is. Very important – keep the cages clean. That includes the food bowls, perches, everything. A bird can get very sick very fast in a dirty cage. Got it?"

"That's it?"

"Mostly. You'll pick up things as you go along, but those are the basics."

What a marvelous woman. Mary never wastes time or oxygen on nonsense, just says what needs to be said. I've made good use of the education and resources she provided, and I'm glad to have her on my rolodex. Even happier to be on hers.

We'll watch out for daydreaming high school students as we turn north here at Rt. 58. "How are you doing, Maggie? We'll walk after I see Miss Kitty, okay?" Kendal is a so-called retirement community, with much of the woods and wetlands left intact. The trails there should be pleasant, while the weather holds. I always enjoy walking there, but Maggie has other favorites.

Before I understood Maggie, and when the business was just getting started, I seldom took her with me. Left alone, she would stage a protest by emptying the kitchen wastebasket. I would return to the house to find a mess, and this wasn't just an emptied wastebasket. It was more like an art installation. All paper items were chewed into slimy wads, and non-paper, like cellophane or foil, was torn into tiny glistening bits. These specially treated pieces of trash were scattered over the kitchen floor, into the dining room, living room, and halfway up the stairs. She wasn't after food, because I compost everything possible, and I keep any meat papers in the freezer until trash day. She wasn't doing this out of boredom, either. I know because one day I started to leave, but ran back into the house to get something. She was already "at work." Maggie was just making a statement. She wanted to go with me. I would pretend to be angry as I cleaned up the mess, thinking that would make a difference. She would sit in the kitchen watching me, her eyes sparkling with unspent mischief.

One day after a wastebasket episode, I looked at Maggie and realized that my sweet girl was essentially a grown woman. In dog years, she was in her early thirties. So, okay, this young adult female surely had opinions, yearnings, and ideas. I had no right to claim she was my best friend if I didn't make every effort to understand her and to acknowledge what was important to her. I was hardly her best friend if I expected that she should merely accommodate me and always live up to my expectations of what a dog should be or do. I loved her more than my own life, but I sometimes treated her as if she were a nuisance. I had trained her in the basic commands that well-behaved dogs must learn, but that was scratching the surface of what our relationship could become. My ego had prevented me from seeing myself as anything but her teacher, trainer, and owner. Ha! Maggie was expending lots of effort trying to get me to see things differently. Perhaps this was the moment when I recognized what she had always known, that I was supposed to be her student. My assumptions and worn-out notions had to be torn up, just like the kitchen trash.

CHAPTER 3

7:45am Miss Kitty

Okay, here's our parking lot. Kendal Drive goes around the place in a big circle, and missing the correct parking lot is a pain. I'll roll the windows down a bit, so Maggie can enjoy the sights and sounds, particularly the wonderful honking screeches of the Canada geese. "Maggie, I'll see you soon."

The cottage is close. Now we get to see the last of some beautiful gardens. This place is known for having many accomplished gardeners. Trumpet vine and morning glories climb the pillars, and purple asters and marigolds are still holding their own. If you gawk too much at the flowers, you're likely to brain yourself on a hanging basket or wind chime. In a few more weeks, the place will start to look rather stark.

Here we are. I cherish my time with Miss Kitty, for her human doesn't go away often. She's a dignified senior cat, with the ability to be sweet and cantankerous at the same time, as you will see. "Miss Kitty? Where are you, dear? Ah, here's my sweet friend." Poor thing, I don't know if it's arthritis or an old injury of some kind that makes her walk like Quasimodo. Her head is permanently turned to one side, as if she's trying to look over her shoulder. She has to come to a full stop to look up at me, or she falls over. Her estimated age is eighteen, and she has had a very good life so far. Her human says she was quite beautiful in her youth and was called Black Velvet. Now, that may be a reference to her coat quality, or it might be a reference to those sexy Black Velvet Whiskey billboards of long ago. Probably both.

"Let's get that motor going. Oh, you love to have your head scratched. There it is, the purr that sputters to life like an old tractor. Keep it going, kitty cat. There, now it's steady."

"Okay, my dear, let's change the water bowl and get you some food. Oh, sure, it's looks as though you've gargled in the water again. And your food bowl is empty. Some little girl loves to eat. Yes, that same vice destroyed my schoolgirl figure, too. I know all about it. At least you don't blow crumbs all over, as some voracious eaters do."

Some cats shake their heads when they're eating, and so food crumbs are everywhere. Miss Kitty is relatively neat, perhaps because of her stiff neck. Speaking of messes versus lack thereof, how's the pan? The pan is down this short hallway, and is the biggest one I've ever seen. I think it may have come from a construction site, something to mix mortar in perhaps. It looks to be about two feet long, and maybe twenty inches wide. Probably ten inches high. Miss Kitty's human doesn't like to clean it out very often, so size was her solution. That works well for one cat. I wouldn't recommend it for multiple –cat households. There – we'll take this nasty stuff to the trash room on the way to the parking lot. I'll sanitize the pan the day before Miss Kitty's human comes home, so she won't have to face that chore for a while.

Here's something I've learned as a pet sitter that no one talks about. Everyone with an indoor cat knows about it, though. People who design cat pans and people who design cat pan scoopers never communicate with each other. Many cat lovers who try to play along with the kitty accessory industry end up buying many scoopers, sometimes for just one pan. Often they get caught up in a particular kind of madness that compels them to buy bigger and bigger scoopers. Size is not the problem. Let me tell you what I have found. Forget about scoopers. Think housewares. The best scoopers are slotted spoons, ladles, skimmers and strainers. Use an old utensil from the kitchen drawer and treat yourself to a new ergonomically correct one for cooking.

Long before I ever thought I might become a pet sitter, I had the experience of going out of town and having a good friend take care of my cats. She had begged me to let her take care of them, and, after all, the darlin' had a degree in zoology. Overqualified, right? I came home after five days to a house full of frantic cats and a bed adorned with a dried-out hairball. Turns out my friend didn't realize just how time consuming the commitment would be. "I rushed through the door every day and threw food at them. And I certainly didn't have time to run around the house and inspect for mishaps." Well, of course not. Pet care is difficult and time consuming. After all, she was doing me a favor. There was nothing to forgive, but I never forgot.

As it happens, my old friend did me a big favor, quite different from the one we had agreed upon. I took away from that experience the feeling of finding the hairball on my bed when I was road weary. I had to take the time to strip and re-make the bed instead of falling into it. As for my cats, I learned what can happen when they get very little attention for several days. Mine became quite anxious, although most of them calmed down within a day or two of my return. The great Carolyn, my eldest cat at the time, began howling, although she had never done this before. She kept staring at me as though she couldn't believe her eyes. She had spells of keening like a banshee for about five months.

This brings me to why I'll be changing this gigantic pan before Miss Kitty's human returns. I want my clients to come home to relaxed pets and clean homes. Anything less is unacceptable.

Oh, my, a cricket. I hear it, but where is it? He's the first one I've heard indoors this season. It's the time for the poor things to seek warmth, reminding me of that old story about the ant and the grasshopper. "Mr. Cricket, you've chosen a safe place. Miss Kitty can't chase you down, my dear."

Ah, there he is, halfway under the baseboard in the hallway. He'll just starve to death slowly, I suppose. I'd help if I could, but I think his season is over. Let's check on our girl.

"Hey, Miss Kitty. How was breakfast? How about a back rub?" She'll just let me sit here on the floor with her, rubbing her back and neck. She'd be happy with a full-time masseuse. Once in a while she'll allow me to brush her, but I won't try that this morning.

Now, here's something I feel obligated to do. I'll reach as sneakily as I can for the clippers in my pocket. I always tell her human that I'll have Miss Kitty's claws trimmed before she returns. The first time I made that pledge, I didn't fully appreciate what I was getting into. Don't think I wasn't warned. In fact, let me take the time to state that I was told she was one difficult customer if anyone tried to groom her in any fashion. This is in sharp contrast to those pet stewards who lie outright or fail to disclose unfortunate behaviors in their pets. Miss Kitty is a very good friend of mine, right up until she sees the clippers. Then she's a teeth-snapping gator-cat.

Here's how we do it. I have a total of seven days to trim Miss Kitty's claws, so my goal is to do at least two each day. Some days I may not clip any, and on lucky days I make up for it. Her claws are so large and long, they protrude a bit, giving me some advantage.

"Let's pet our girl. Well, that was fast. You dropped to the floor in a second. Oh, sure. I know better than to touch that great expanse of belly." What a wonderful difference between dogs and cats- when dogs show their bellies, they're inviting a tummy rub. Not so with a cat. When a cat shows her belly, she's saying, "I trust you enough to relax this much." Accept the compliment and respect the likely boundaries that go with it. Don't touch unless you're on the most familiar of terms. It's purely up to the individual cat.

Any human who won't accept that may initially lose a little blood, and eventually the cat's friendship.

Miss Kitty's eyes close and her claws come out as she "makes bread" in the air. That's my opening, and – gotta be quick – nope. Missed it. Ha! Got one. Miss Kitty's startled expression goes to her paw, then to my face. She flashes a look that says I have betrayed our friendship and she will never trust me again. I feel terrible for one or two seconds, until her eyes close again. Within moments she relaxes as though nothing happened. My decision to clip another is based on whether the tip of her tail has begun to tap the floor. She's still relaxed. I'll rub her back and her side for a while longer.

As casual as this little grooming session may be, it serves more than one purpose. Claws in an older animal can thicken, and even curl into the pad. Animals will tolerate a lot of pain, keeping you unaware if you haven't checked their paws lately. Infection comes in the next stage, and then you have a real mess. It's amazing how bad it can get before your cat begins to limp. Miss Kitty's claws don't seem to grow that way, at least not yet. And right now, the tip of her tail is barely moving. I take that as a sign of relaxation, so I'll go for just one more claw. There it is, and it's the thumb. Got it! Terrific.

"What a good girl. At this rate, we'll be done by the end of the week."

Basic routine brushing works miracles. You don't need any special talent, just a little patience and enough devotion to brush your pet regularly. Hey, how often do you brush your own hair? How often do you bathe? I once asked a groomer about brushing pets, and she went into the most intimidating lecture about having just the right table, the correct tools, and heaven knows what. I'm thinking that's what she needs – and then some- as a professional, but an ordinary person with a pet doesn't. I would suggest finding a brush that's comfortable yet effective for your pet's coat type. You'll know if it's right, because there won't be any tangles forming over time. You should be able to get through the coat, but not to irritate the skin. I give out combs with rotating teeth to my clients dealing with long-haired pets. Great invention, combs that don't tug but that gently remove knots. I often get reports from clients that their cats "ask" to be combed with them.

"Okay, Miss Kitty, let's shift gears now and brush you a little. No more sneaky clippers. Oh, yes, isn't that nice?" Her coat isn't long, but it's thick. The brush I like for her has firm bristles with rubber tips. My goal is to brush all over if possible. It can make a dramatic difference to both skin and coat, and that isn't the only benefit. The interaction between you is worthwhile all by itself. After all, we're talking about companion animals. They want attention from you. Beyond that, you may discover those important things no one wants to find and that your pet would just as soon you didn't know. Remember that domesticated animals still have at least one toe in the wild. It's their inclination to hide weakness or sickness until they can't hide it any more. While brushing them, you may find lumps, bumps, cysts, or sore spots indicating the early stage of a problem. When it happens, get your sweetie to the vet.

"Miss Kitty, this is going well, but I wonder if we should try a brief outing. It may rain later." She's loving this, especially on the back of her neck and near her tail. She's a bit too old and stiff to reach everything herself for spot cleaning.

"Good kitty. No more clipping until tomorrow. Let's go outside." We'll go through the enclosed patio to the grassy area beyond. She loves it, and never goes very far. She wears herself out sniffing and evaluating darn nearly every blade of grass just beyond the patio doors. Actually, an enclosed patio is enough for many cats. "What? You don't want to go? You're going to lie down out here on the patio. Okay, then." I wonder if she senses the coming rain. Clearly, Miss Kitty is settling in for a personal grooming session and a post-breakfast nap. Amazing, that as stiff as she is, she can still wash her own back leg. We'll leave her to that task.

"Sweetie, I'll leave you in peace. I love you. See you later."

Let's not forget the bag of goo from the pan. We'll quickly drop that off in the trash room on the way to the car. Some people would be surprised to know what a weak stomach I actually have for the janitorial aspect of this work.

Maggie will be ready for her morning walk, and Kendal has some pretty trails. I may have to talk her into it, since she has strong preferences about where she walks. I don't know how she became so opinionated. "Hey, Mag. Let's stretch our legs before I have to walk Folly. And why are you in my seat? C'mon, pretty girl." Yes, this all sounds like blah, blah, blah. That's okay. I'm not in training mode and I'm not trying to give her a command. I'm just talking, and this way I'm not talking to myself. It's one of the least discussed benefits of having a dog.

"Which way? Okay." I guess we're going to cross the street here and walk around the rose garden. Maggie can't possibly care about roses, although I do. Rose gardens remind me of my grandmother, who had a backyard garden of nearly seventy different varieties. She fussed with them in the evening after work, as a way to unwind. Her roses were nothing like these, for what we have here are those highly fragrant and painfully prickly heirloom roses. Every bush produces a distinctive and complex fragrance. Their season is about done at this point, but in the height of summer, this is a lovely place to linger. The bushes, arranged in a kind of double horseshoe, wrap around me as I sit on this bench.

"What is it, Maggie?" Someone must have anointed this area, or maybe that loveable skunk has been by. If we're here at dusk, we'll see lots of wildlife. I envy Maggie her interest in this place. She doesn't rely on sentimental references for interpretation of what she senses, but lives fully in the present. Her behavior reminds me that the physical world is alive with smells and sounds that my dull human senses know nothing about. She knew long before I did, relying as I do primarily on my sight, that this place is populated by geese, ducks, muskrats, stray and feral cats, herons, red-wing blackbirds, goldfinches, and I don't know what else.

I became aware many years ago that my pampered indoor cats and the stray and feral neighborhood cats seem to define collectively how they use and travel through territory. There seem to be small areas that belong to individuals, pathways that are used communally, and intersections that are constantly negotiated. In the house, many of these invisible lines and zones become habituated after a while, and change only when the feline population changes or the furniture is rearranged. Then the re-negotiation may be fierce. Outdoors, the strays have the additional task of working together to defend the larger territory against intruders, feline and otherwise. I have never known how large that outdoor territory is, but I have seen "my" strays blocks away from my yard. These observations of cats' use of territory constitute my paltry understanding of this behavior among animals.

Maggie must know well the pathways and intersections of the creatures I don't see. I figure she can detect how recently they've been by, whether they are well or ill, hungry or fed, frightened or seeking a mate. I assume this is why she makes such a study of vegetation, particularly around ponds. Their environment is more complicated than that of the stray cats I've watched. For wild animals there are the additional considerations of access to food and shelter, and who is the natural enemy of whom. Daylight is necessary for some animals, while others are nocturnal. I like to think that some behaviors are negotiated, but opportunism, aggression and cunning must play a large part. Those traits have certainly served humankind all too well.

All of this runs through my mind as Maggie moves slowly from one blade of grass to another. You see, we cling to a myth about having a big dog we can jog along the beach with; walking our big dog every day will help to keep us fit. I walk a lot of dogs, and most of them prefer to mosey. Maggie can mosey like nobody's business. When I want a workout, I go to an aerobics class.

"C'mon, Mag, let's go east to that pond that has the tiny island in the middle. Maybe we'll see the heron." An unrelenting wind comes off that pond that's now behind us, and I prefer having it to my back. In a few minutes, we won't feel it. As we move eastward toward the pond and surrounding trees, the air is relatively still. The sound of the wind will be replaced by bird song. Except for the "tweeee" of the redwing blackbird, I don't know one bird vocalization from another, yet I am aware of a variety of birdsong. These sounds remind me constantly of how little I know of the riches surrounding me. Maggie is just marching right along. Oh, nuts, I had to say that. "What do you see, sweetheart? Oh, sure, a rabbit. Well, we can watch her as long as you like." Maggie's complete lack of prey drive assures me that she will never break into a frenzied chase. She's fascinated by animals, and especially by anything that flies. As a puppy, she would try to chase birds, planes and helicopters.

"You're hardly stopping at all right now. Not that I'm complaining." She walks to heel so beautifully when it suits her. It seems to be second nature now. I remember when I thought she was an obstreperous puppy that would never learn anything. Then at about ten months of age, she seemed suddenly to do everything right. A co-worker at the time told me that Labs are like gifted children, seemingly unable to pay attention because they are actually paying attention to everything at once. At some point in their development, they learn to filter incoming information. That seems to be what happened with Maggie.

A few years ago, when I decided to adopt a dog, I weighed the same factors most people do. I thought puppies were adorable, but their energy level was overwhelming and the prospect of training one was, well, overwhelming. I grew up with dogs, but in a very different time. I didn't know the first thing about what a puppy needed. An adult dog from rescue sounded like a good idea, until people started telling me that I would just be taking on the result of someone else's mistakes. As with many choices, pros and cons existed on both sides. The more I talked to people and listened to their "advice," the more uncertain I was. All I could do was to start getting up close and personal with a few dogs, and yes, I was going to brace myself against some puppies, too.

Every time I answered an ad placed by people with a dog they wanted to unload, I told myself I would do nothing rash. First I met a Rottweiler that was being dumped by his third family. He seemed sweet, sad, and worn down with disappointment. He would barely look at me. A mixed breed dog that had been abandoned at a kennel wouldn't look at me either. The kennel owner brought him out to the lobby so I could meet him. When I spoke to him, he leaned away from me. I can't remember all the adult dogs I considered, but it was an utterly soul-crushing experience. The world of animal rescue began to come into focus for me as the work of the saints. If I hadn't been so busy with my own mid-life crisis – recognizing all my flaws – I would have begun railing at the outrageous shortcomings of human beings and their nearly criminal negligence of animals. Never mind abuse.

In the midst of those encounters with damaged dogs, I decided to live dangerously. I had always dreamed of having a chocolate Lab, and an ad in the local paper caught my eye. A breeder was taking reservations on a litter of eight Labrador retrievers, four black and four chocolate. I worked up my courage and told myself that no matter what happened, I wasn't making a commitment. I was just going to look. I just wanted the experience. I wasn't going to do anything rash.

After a quick call to my vet for advice, I knew I wanted to be able to see both parents onsite, as well as the paperwork regarding purebred status. I knew so little about dog breeding, the AKC, and even the breed I thought I loved so much. In hindsight, I realize that I didn't ask the important questions. I was unprepared and uneducated with respect to the task at hand, perhaps because I was still resisting the idea of adopting a puppy.

I walked through the front door of the breeder's modest home, then had to get past a nervous black Lab that the breeder's husband identified as the father. The breeder was a plump, cheerful woman who beckoned me into the kitchen to watch the six-week-old puppies having supper. They were eating some kind of semi-moist glop in a sort of circular trough, and getting it all over their faces and paws. The woman and I talked about the puppies and their parents, when the pups would be available and the cost. She obviously had done all this before. She continued chattering happily, proceeding to clean off the squirming puppies as each one strayed from the food bowl. She seemed to have endless patience.

They had been born on Valentine's Day and the breeder said they would be ready by the middle of April. Not twelve weeks? No, she said with a smile, the mother dog had had other litters, and it always seemed that they had learned everything from her that they needed in eight weeks. Hmmm. This would have been a good place to ask a question, or protest, but I just didn't know enough. The vet had said that twelve weeks was best, but that eight weeks had become standard because of good old-fashioned greed. I didn't ask how many litters the dog had had. Such a nice woman wouldn't overbreed this beautiful Lab, right? I watched as she placed each puppy back in the huge whelping box that took up most of the dining room. The woman could sense that I was vaguely uncomfortable, and she had her own reason for being frustrated.

"It's too bad they just ate. They'll all fall asleep now, and there's nothing we can do about that. As of now, we have reservations on two males. See the two cuties there with yellow kitty collars? They're spoken for." I saw flashes of yellow as most of the puppies waddled toward the back of the box to pile on top of each other and up against their already sleeping mother. "No one has wanted a chocolate one yet, so you'd have your pick. Maybe if you came back tomorrow, an hour earlier than today. You could see them in action." I was in sales myself at the time, but anyone could have felt her eagerness to have money in her pocket and her dining room back.

I thought I should get a sense of their personalities, and they hadn't yet done anything to differentiate themselves from one another. So far I had seen them chowing down like little piggies, then I had seen them resisting the washcloth. Now they were headed for dreamland. Except for one.

As I made small talk with the breeder about what to look for in assessing disposition – in case I actually came back - a chocolate puppy came over to us. I leaned down to pet her. Her tail was wagging and she was almost jumping, as if she wanted to get out of the box. The breeder laughed. "You're allowed to pick her up."

The radiating warmth and wriggling energy from that little dog's body took me back instantly to my childhood. I must have been about eight years old the last time I had this experience. At that stage of my life, my own energy level was puppy-like, with long summer days filled with bike riding, tree climbing and mindless running for its own sake. As an adult I expected to feel overwhelmed by a puppy's energy, and here was that feeling. She certainly was cute. Every new creature is, I told myself.

The puppy and I smelled each other's faces while the breeder explained to me why the females cost almost thirty percent more than the males. I wasn't really listening. The woman told me the puppy's name was Bitsie because she was the smallest chocolate, and in fact the smallest of the litter. I hadn't noticed that, but I did notice an alarming sound. The puppy was falling asleep in my arms, wrapped in the warmth of my wool pea coat. As she inhaled, she made a slight wheezing sound. This was my out.

"Do you hear that? Does she have a breathing problem? I hope it isn't contagious." I wasn't about to take on a sick dog. No, sir.

"Oh, no." The woman looked at me with disbelief. "Haven't you ever heard that before? That's a happy puppy sound."

Oh, sure. She had the well-rehearsed comeback, and once again, I had nothing to say. There was the off-chance that she was right. If so, that grumbling breathy sound could be endearing. Otherwise, the pup probably had some type of canine TB. How was I going to know the difference? Well, I came to my senses. After all, I was the tough one who wasn't going home with a dog anyway, right? No promises, no deposit down, no commitment. This was just a foray into puppy land to see what it was all about. Besides, I still had other adult dogs to see. Whether she was well or sickly, she would likely become someone else's concern.

Over the next week or so, I looked at a few more adult dogs looking for new homes. Of course, they weren't actually looking. They were going to be the last to know about their change in circumstances. During my meetings with them, I could tell that they knew something was up.

They seemed sad, anxious, uncertain. My parents weren't always crazy about me, but they never turned to me to say, "Pack your things. You'll be moving, just as soon as another family comes along to take you in." I wasn't always crazy about my folks, either, but they were mine. We belonged to each other for the long haul, and any breach of that was something close to a sin, perhaps even a crime. When do we take seriously our role as stewards of domesticated animals? And how did these people actually feel about what they were doing? Were they uneasy, embarrassed, disappointed in themselves? I couldn't get a reading, but for the most part the humans expressed vague disappointment in the dogs. Nuisance barkers, impossible to train, chased the cat, not good with kids, allergies, blah, blah, blah. I'd know what to say to those people now. Oh, boy, would I. At the time, I merely suspected they were justifying going back on a sacred promise.

I hope you understand I was afraid of being one of those people myself. I hadn't had a dog of my own in my adult life. I was going to need one kind of patience for a second-hand dog and another for a rambunctious puppy. Did I have enough patience of any kind? I don't suffer fools gladly, but I can be nearly endlessly patient for anyone who needs for me to be. I would have to help the broken-hearted dog learn to trust again, and I wasn't sure I was the best example of my species to be doing that. Then I would have to gradually back her off of some deeply ingrained inappropriate behaviors, replacing them with better ones. We're talking about training skills I did not yet possess.

If I adopted a puppy, that commitment, too, would be forever, no matter what. I thought back on those people I met who were trying to unload their dogs, and I was damned if I would be one of them. I can still recall their unease, whatever the cause of it. Speaking for myself, I had had enough of personal failure. Taking on a puppy would mean studying training books like a monk, then following what I'd learned like a true believer. That puppy's heart and spirit would be protected like the Holy Grail. And since I was never going to rise to such a standard, that settled that. Well, almost.

Several weeks after my search for a dog began, and two weeks after meeting Bitsie at the breeder's, I was out of ideas. Other puppies of other breeds were being advertised, along with the same sad classifieds for unwanted adult dogs. I didn't want to see those adult dogs any more. In retrospect, they reflected the sense of sorrow and loss I myself was trying to rise above. I had given up many long-held illusions and had said goodbye to the profession I loved. I was thinking about that puppy, and for the most selfish of reasons. I wanted to be re-charged by that happy puppy energy. I would call the breeder, and with any luck, Bitsie would already be spoken for. She would be eight weeks old by now, and I could stop this foolishness in its tracks. I wanted her and I knew that there must be a thousand other people more worthy. I needed her, but she did not need me.

Convincing myself that the breeder now had an empty whelping box, I called her number. You could have scraped me off the floor when she said, "Bitsie is waiting for you." She told me that she and two black males were still available.

I asked, "Why do you say she's waiting for me?" You can ignore people when they talk nonsense or you can get to the bottom of it.

The woman swore that whenever a prospective adopter wanted to see her, Bitsie would go to the back of the whelping box, face the wall, and sit down. If anyone managed to pick her up, she would stiffen like road kill. "You're the only person she liked," the woman cooed. Yeah, right. I remembered the funny sound the puppy made in her throat, and I wondered if people were rejecting her because of it. Once again, this seemingly simple woman had me at a disadvantage. Remember? I had called in order to hear that the dog was gone and I could move on. But, no, the woman still had the dog. Now what? She went on, "When would you like to see her again?" Okay. I would go one more time, be tough one more time, and I would probably make an issue of that strange breathing problem. That would do it. Out the door.

At 2:00 that afternoon, I stepped into the breeder's living room. From there, I saw two large handsome men kneeling in front of the whelping box. One of them was holding a black puppy. The other man was trying to get the other puppies, one black and one chocolate, to come to him. The woman explained that these off-duty cops were duck hunters, hoping to take two of the remaining three puppies. One man apparently had his new puppy. At the woman's urging, I watched closely. The second fellow was having no luck with Bitsie, who did exactly what the woman had described over the phone. She went as far away as she could get and showed the man her little round back. Oh, my.

Of course, I can't explain what happened next. Something made me call out, "Hey, puppy!" I moved quickly across the room, startling the men as well as myself. Bitsie's little head snapped around and her tail started wagging. She ran to the front of the box and started jumping up and down. I picked up that warm, wriggling sweetheart and she started making that funny noise. Maybe it truly was a happy puppy sound. I'm not going to walk around this beautiful pond on a September morning in the full light of the sun, trying to explain how animals choose us. I have no explanation. I just knew in that moment with rock-solid certainty that that little dog was mine and I was hers.

I never uttered the name "Bitsie." My girl would need a beautiful and dignified name she could grow into, and one that meant something to me every time I said it. I named her for my great-grandmother, Maggie Carter, a legendary woman known to be warm, strong, and wise. And because of my puppy's birthday and her hook in my heart, she became Maggie Valentine.

"Hey, Mag, let's move on, okay?" She makes me crazy when she finds one blade of grass that requires a lengthy analysis, an examination from several angles. Just when it seems she's ready to start walking, I realize she's just shifting her weight so she can stand in one spot longer, doing what I've come to think of as her dog work. We can behave like two old fussbudgets, with my scolding and her dirty looks. I have been known to give her a tug, and Maggie has been known to tug back! There are times when she will not be rushed. I usually give in. I am sometimes rewarded in places such as this with a heron sighting or the discovery of a wildflower I hadn't noticed before and cannot readily identify. If I weren't standing around waiting for Maggie, I just might have missed it.

J. R. Ackerley, in *My Dog Tulip*, says, "Dogs read the world through their noses and write their history in urine." Yep.

"Okay, Maggie, we need to move on. Paying customers await. Folly will be expecting me, and I won't let the sweet boy down. Let's get back to the car, my dear."

Maggie will sleep now, until I come back. It's just short of 9:00, so we're still on schedule. I always look forward to seeing Folly, the only standard poodle I have ever taken care of.

The cottage we're headed for is just to the left of this gorgeous garden. The ornamental cherry tree has more and more flowers around it every year. The ajuga is spreading, slowly choking out the grass, something I have no use for anyway. I keep meaning to ask the gardeners for the source of their irises. The season for them is past, but I remember how the brilliant corals, blues and purples put my ordinary yellow irises to shame. Their Shasta daisies, something that will not grow in my yard, are so large and tall every year. The bright yellow coreopsis is still blooming, as if it were July, and a nice complement to the deep purple asters.

CHAPTER 4

9:00am Marian's Folly

Okay, here's Folly's cottage. We'll knock and go in. "Anyone home? Hey, Folly! Where's your human? Oh, that's right; she's gone for the day. Maybe we'll see her later. What a good boy. Oh, yes, you are." His black fur is so soft and curly, and his new groomer does a great job with the cut. Mostly short all over, pompom tail, and long on the ears. A kennel cut, I believe. What a handsome boy. "Hey, buddy, did you finish your breakfast? Looks like it, and you have fresh water. Okay. Let's get out of here." We use a choker, but I can't for the life of me understand why. Maybe just an old habit going back to his puppyhood. He walks to heel perfectly.

We'll pass my favorite garden again and go left this time, toward that windmill. The pond there, on the northeast corner of the Kendal campus, usually has an unrelenting wind coming off of it. The day is warm enough now that we can stand it. "Folly, you are such a joy to walk with." Apparently he had had no training when he first "retired" here. He had been walked over the years by a series of neighborhood kids. He learned to walk to heel for me just after his family moved here. He needed about five minutes to understand what I wanted from him.

"Sit." All clear. "Okay." We'll cross here while we have a chance. Standard poodles are a great breed, but I hope that doesn't become widely known. When breeds become popular, something bad usually happens. With poodles, a couple of hurdles keep them from being sought after. The grooming requirements are daunting for most people. Poodles should probably see a groomer every four weeks, although I know of another poodle here who sees a groomer every six weeks because his humans have learned how to do touch-ups in between appointments. Every poodle's human has to do at least a little maintenance each day of that marvelous curly coat. It's like human hair, growing endlessly and needing daily brushing. That's the price for fur that probably won't make you sneeze.

Poodles are both smart and emotional, so they react poorly to punishment. That may be where they get a long-standing reputation for being "nippy." Fortunately, training methods today are based on positive reinforcement and reward, rather than the harsher corrections of earlier times. That's good news for more than just poodles. Folly's human says she housetrained him by securing a paper towel with a garden stake in the side yard. The towel had been used to clean up after his first "accident" in the house. It turned out to be the only time he soiled in the house, because he went where he smelled the stinky towel after that. That story squares nicely with my experience with leash training him. "Yes, you are just the best boy."

When I say poodles are emotional, I mean seriously. Folly would not eliminate for the first forty-eight hours he lived at Kendal. Other dogs had already anointed the Kendal grounds, so Folly was apparently intimidated. I had to rush him to the vet to be catheterized before his bladder burst! The vet we saw that day was completely understanding of Folly's state of mind, confirming my belief that his sensitivity could complicate his adjustment to his new home. The vet penciled in an appointment for the following morning, in case Folly's "reverse incontinence" continued. I thought for a moment about the effective stinky towel method from his puppyhood, but knew we couldn't cover the Kendal campus with bits of soiled toweling to signal permission. Folly liked the vet, who was actually a lot like Folly. He was handsome, dark-haired, smart and gentle. We didn't need the next morning's appointment, and we never saw that vet again. After that intervention, Folly made an immediate adjustment to his situation.

"Let's cross over here, my sweet, and we'll try to stay out of the mud." As we move north a bit and east, we'll walk just briefly around this big pond before we pick up the trail. The Canada geese are likely to choose this place in the spring for nesting purposes. We wouldn't be able to get anywhere near these ponds at that time of year, but we're safe now from the geese's honking din. Instead, we may hear just an occasional wet "plunk" as an amphibian hides from our moving shadows.

I don't mean to suggest that poodles are exceptional in any negative way. Every breed has behavioral traits going back to the original purpose for the breed, and every breed has its own grooming requirements. These are some of the factors we all must consider when choosing a dog. Some other considerations are trainability, energy level, size, and potential health problems. Of course, some of that may blur a bit when dealing with mixed breeds. Then there's that funny-faced sweetie at the pound – well, let's be honest – maybe the best strategy is to make a short list of traits you *won't* accept. Aggression, for example. Shoot, I don't know. I've already told you how I ended up with Maggie Dog. If you want a dog, you just may be lucky enough for a dog to let you take him home. Then the onus is on you to be worthy.

"Let's watch where we're walking, young man." I always feel conflicted about letting a dog have a good time on his walk while trying to keep him from turning into a mud puppy.

Pets as old as Folly or Miss Kitty end up in shelters all the time. The senior dogs and cats I know are such lovable characters, but I know when older pets go up for adoption, their chances are slim of finding a new home. Someone I've worked for has several old dogs that she's taken out of the Animal Protective League in Cleveland. She knows dogs, and can walk into such a heartbreaking facility and pick out a winner. Her only requirement is that the dog has to be black! Don't ask me why. She has always taken in dogs that are at least eight years old, and makes the last half of their lives a complete spoil-fest. Good food, clean beds, and lots of tummy rubs. They don't ask for more.

Selecting a cat may be easier. Friendly cats reach for you through the bars. We all know how reserved cats can be when feeling stressed or uncertain. I've seen them in those cold, damp cages at animal shelters. They regard you through narrowed eyes, as they hunch uncomfortably in a corner. When they risk everything to try to touch you, consider yourself chosen. Cats have always found me, depriving me of the chance to go looking for one to adopt. If I ever have the chance, I'll look for an older cat, and I'll hope to be chosen. With my beat-up pet sitter's knees, I don't want a kitten tripping me on his 60-mile-per-hour blast through the house.

Let me say a thing or two about cats and grooming. Miss Kitty and others are next to impossible when it comes to claw trimming. I've raised enough kittens to know that some cats are born that way. Those arm-shredding devils were born with the idea that anyone's messing with their paws and feet is just too darn personal. Brushing is another matter. Even when you start with an adult cat, you can succeed in convincing her that brushing is a pleasurable experience. You'll see in the brush just how much fur your cat would have had to eat if you had not intervened. Long-haired cats have to be brushed and combed daily. There's no getting out of it. If you cannot do this yourself, or are unwilling to do so, get your kitty to a groomer on a regular schedule.

"Okay, Folly, let's cross here again." Back at the road, we'll have to cross to pick up the sidewalk. We'll walk south to the service road, and see what appeals to us once we get there. To the right of us is a farmer's field with thistles growing along the edge. At certain times of year, driving slowly along here is imperative, not to mention breathtaking, when flocks of goldfinches swirl in front of the car. Folly ignores them. He isn't predatory in the least. When I asked his human way back when about his habits, she said that he liked to "chase after white trash." For some reason, I knew immediately what she meant. Folly will lunge after any kind of paper, although understandably he likes food wrappers best.

That field on our right is a bit of a mystery. Soy beans grow in it every year, but I never see anyone working it. The field to the north of Kendal is much larger and is part of an active farm. It's on the far side of a huge man-made ridge known as Kendal Mountain. Often at this time of year, people gather on top of the ridge to watch the harvesting. I've stood there myself, although I have to figure the guys in those air conditioned tractor cabs are wondering what the fascination is with monotonous, dusty, spine-busting work. I just have to say this. People may think that what I do for a living is superfluous, and they're right. What you do probably is, too. Off-color jokes aside, the oldest occupation is farming, and one of the few necessary ones. Face it – after food production, everything else is embellishment.

Oh, right, back to long-haired cats. At least as challenging as poodles in terms of care. There's a local groomer who is on a life-long campaign to get cat owners to do a better job of grooming their own cats. One day when I was in her shop using the do-it-yourself dog bath for a client's dog, I saw what looked like a vast collection of wigs on a 20-foot-high wall. They were white, silver, black, orange, blond, and gray. When I stood at the counter to pay, I finally saw the tell-tale stripes in the orange "wig." Then I realized that under each one was a surname. I felt a chill. I said, "These aren't cat pelts, I hope." The groomer shot me a look, perhaps irritated at first, but then she smiled.

"Come closer. I'd like you to admire my work." The groomer invited me to walk behind the counter. She took a bundle of gray fur down for me to examine. Up close and in my hands, it was like a small and surprisingly heavy rug made of knots. Clearly, this woman was so talented with clippers that she was able to remove a long-haired cat's hopelessly matted coat all in one piece. There must have been fifteen of them on the wall, with plenty of room for more. I started to think whether I had brushed either Shadow or Sammy the day before, then squelched the thought. A guilty blush would have made me unworthy of further conversation, and I had more questions.

I said gingerly, "I noticed the names." Was this woman crazy?

The woman grinned. "Oh, yes, after I shave the cats, I scold the owners. For those who will listen, I give short lessons in care of the coat, and make recommendations for tools appropriate for each cat. In any case, the name goes on the wall. I call it the 'wall of shame.' I just hope that these particular pet owners will go and sin no more. Can you imagine how much pain you would be in if your hair was matted up against your scalp like an old hat? Then imagine such a condition covering your entire body. Then imagine *being* a cat, a creature for whom meticulous grooming is essential. Honestly." She waved her hands in the air, in a gesture of frustration.

I had to add something. "How do you think the cats feel when they've been shaved?"

"Ha! These cats had to feel relieved of the pain at first. But, you know, what could be more humiliating for such a creature than to be without her natural covering? Let's not even talk about the vulnerability."

One more observation about grooming and this groomer in particular. A different groomer once told me that many groomers are abusive. Yes, this was a shocking statement coming from someone in the business. I have never found anyone else in that industry who might support or refute that opinion. She said that the only way to know how a groomer treats a pet is for the client to be able to watch. She stated, in no uncertain terms, that if a groomer refuses to let a client watch, the client should take her business elsewhere. The "wall of shame" groomer? Well, she has a work area with three Plexiglas walls, and beyond them, a semi-circle of chairs just a few feet from where she stands. Talk about transparency! That's my kind of animal lover.

"Folly, forgive me, sweetie, while I pull you close. We have to get through the employee parking lot, you know. Yes, my dear, we don't take their wild driving personally, even though any resulting injuries would hurt just as much."

Visitors park here, but mostly we see employees running late, careening into the place playing "beat the clock." Alternatively, we see employees leaving, evidently ecstatic beyond reason to be going home. All a body can do is get out of the way. "That's what we're doing. Right, Folly dog? 'Cuz we're going to live to enjoy this again tomorrow."

The lot is quiet now. This is not a time for a changing of the guard, but we're always on the lookout for strays. "Folly, here's what we'll do. Let's cut around the swimming pool." I was thinking we'd go through the center of the building and pick up a dog biscuit at the reception desk. "Sweetie, I forgot who was on the other end of the leash. You don't like treats." Having a Lab myself, it's easy to forget that some dogs are self-regulating. Maggie will eat anything any time, and not just food. It seems that some breeds are not that way. Standard poodles, Dobermans, and German shepherds tend to be lean. I have seen dogs of those breeds walk away from food or refuse treats. Folly is a long way from his scavenger heritage.

"Oh, shoot, let's cut through anyway. There's no easy way to get around this massive building. Besides, I'll get to show you off." We'll slip in through the back way. Walking down through the main hallway can be a wonderful social opportunity, for Folly as well as the residents. He likes the attention, and some of the people here are long-time dog fans. One lady throws her arms around his neck and fusses over him. Since she's an avid hiker, we see her frequently. Folly now recognizes her at quite a distance, and turns to jelly long before she reaches him. We may see her this morning, or we may see no one. If we encounter someone with a dog, you'll see that Folly does not think of himself as a dog. He'll look upon the other canine with what I'd call pity, then look away.

"That's okay, Folly. I think you just know how handsome you are." Those long poodle legs carry him along with what seems like a Clydesdale prance. No other breed walks that way, as far as I know.

I see a lady at the hairdresser's and someone at the ATM. Just like a little town. "Come on, Folly, to the right. Maybe we'll see an admirer near the mailboxes." It doesn't look promising. Nope. A gathering of three people at the receptionist's desk, and I don't know any of them. True to his nature, Folly is not subtle when he recognizes a friend, and he doesn't seem to know these people either.

"Okay, sweetheart, we tried. Let's get you home for a big drink of water." This set of glass doors is the main entrance, overlooking the pond that separates us from Folly's cottage. "Almost home, mister."

Folly was purchased as a puppy from his owner's hairdresser for twelve dollars. Two different groomers have told me that he is about as close to a perfect specimen as they have ever seen. In his early teens, he has a stunning coat and flawless skin. A groomer had to educate me to the fact that fur on an animal may thin in places with age, as with humans. Also, they may develop skin anomalies, such as moles, cysts, or skin tags. No one knows better than a groomer whether such flaws exist, especially with a high maintenance animal like a poodle. It seems the breeder was "under sanction", and could not sell puppies for the market rate. I know nothing about this stuff, but I am convinced that Folly is a blueblood.

And we're back. "Safe at home, buddy. Yes, you are the best, yes, you are. That's right. Go look for her." He and his human are not that close, really, but he expects her to be here. Dogs are just as much creatures of habit as we are. "What, not here? Let me have a look. Hello? Anyone home? Don't answer if you're not here. See? She won't be home until suppertime, sweetheart." Bedroom, bath, living room and den. Unoccupied. Would I do this in every home? No, but Folly shares his home with an elderly woman who has had a series of health problems. He has taught me to inspect every room. "Folly, you are in charge for the time being. I will see you later, beautiful beast. Remember that I love you."

Now we're off to make a promo call. I don't lock this door. I found it unlocked, and that's the arrangement we have. I leave it as I found it. That's true with many homeowners in this area. All over Lorain County, I locked a few people out of their homes, until I learned to establish a clear understanding about whether to lock or not. I'm astounded at the frequency with which people have told me that they never lock their homes. I'm not stupid about my own safety, and I insist that when clients are leaving town, they lock up. I lock their doors for the duration of their absence. Clients don't know when the wrong person may be watching them pack the car, and I don't want to be the person to find out. For situations such as this, when I know the pet's family is nearby and coming back the same day, I go along with the program.

"Maggie, you're awake. Hello, sweetie. Let's run up the street to drop off some cards, and then we'll go home. You're going to need some water." The car is warming up, so we'll move right along.

CHAPTER 4

9:45am Promotion and call-backs

Today, we're just going a short distance up the road to drop off business cards, but quarterly I set aside a block of time in a day and make sales calls to all the vets and groomers in the area. In any case, this is something I do when I don't really have time. I rarely do this during a slump. A rule for doing promo is to show up walking backwards. In other words, as you go in the door, you have to present yourself as someone who is really busy. I have worked commission sales jobs, and I happen to know that people can smell desperation. Always act busy and happy whether you are or not. Here we are. Let's park and run in.

Another old tried and true law of sales – get out and see the people.

Inside the first set of double doors here is this nice big cork board. We'll slap up some cards, and then give the Miss America wave. "Hey, ladies! Just dropping off cards. Keep doing good works."

Look at this. Always so sad. Every vet hospital bulletin board has a never-ending supply of "lost" flyers for missing dogs and cats. Managing the whereabouts of our pets is part of pet stewardship, but something we don't usually build into the way we live. We fret after the damage is done, and then we're admirably focused and organized as we post flyers all over the neighborhood. We need to microchip our pets, fence our yards, and train cats and dogs to stay away from exit doors. It isn't that they want to leave us; they just know there's more to life and they're going to find it.

Cats that hover near exit doors should experience a sudden loud noise – a stomp or a hiss - just a time or two. (Yes, I know. I already told you about Herbie. I may be a sinner, but I still know how to preach.) Generally, cats are oriented to territory, but a house cat on the loose will behave in one of two ways. Most of those lost meowing darlings can be found cowering near the foundation of the house. The exceptional cat is like my adventure-loving Herbie. He'll take off, returning after about twenty-four hours. He may prowl garages, houses under construction, or anything else dangerous and creepy. He'll come home when he's good and ready, minus his collar. He'll be hungry, filthy, exhausted, and possibly clinging to you for reassurance. My beloved old Carolyn Cat, before she moved indoors, enjoyed creeping around in the house next door when it was being remodeled. The workers encouraged her visits by giving her bits of their lunches. She became trapped in the unheated house in December when the fellows went away for the holidays. After three or four days of unbearable worry, I went looking around the neighborhood, hoping at least to find her corpse. Fortunately, I heard her frantic cries and was able to help her out through an unsecured window.

Dogs are easily trained to stay away from doors, but they are runners by nature. If you lose control of a dog, don't chase him. He'll run even faster, enjoying the sport of it. Here's what often works for me. When a dog escapes my control, I drop to the ground and put my hands to my face. I make loud, dramatic sobbing sounds. I bring my hands down when I feel a snuffling wet nose against them, and then I secure his collar. Being a control freak, I have seldom had to do this.

Just about a year ago, Maggie went wandering, and drama lover that I am, I was sure I had lost her forever. On her usual morning tour of the back yard, she walked toward the back of the property. She came to a stop where the field of brambles began and turned to give me a long look. It was a look I hadn't seen before. She gave me no time to think or react, and so I was dumbstruck when she walked calmly into the overgrowth. She had never done that. Maggie and I had never been separated, except for when she was spayed as a puppy. She had never seemed to want to be anywhere but with me. This was new and scary. I tried to follow her, but couldn't get through the brambles. She wandered into the woods and out of sight. I ran to the house, panic beginning to grow. I couldn't lose my girl. I was almost physically ill by the time I reached the house. What should I do? I could call the police, the pound, and the local animal humane society. Who was I kidding? Who would turn her in? If she showed up on the street, someone would pick her up. She was a gorgeous purebred chocolate. Being a Lab, she'd get into a car with anyone. Every stranger was just a new friend.

I didn't call anyone. As I reached the door, I realized that kids were still walking to school. Kids! Maggie loved them. The high school was down the street and around the corner. Maggie could cut through the woods and come out in the school's parking lot. I jumped in the car and drove slowly, scanning the deep back yards along my street as I went. I thought she might have emerged from the trees. Nope, no dog.

Pulling into the school parking lot, what did I see but a cluster of smiling and laughing students, watching a beautiful brown dog running in circles like a joy-crazed nut. I sat behind the wheel, laughing and crying, not forgetting that I wanted to strangle Maggie for scaring me so badly. I watched her entertain her audience for a while longer, then got out of the car.

"Maggie?" She stopped, her head flipping around at the sound of my voice. Her tail wagged furiously, and her expression seemed to say "What are *you* doing here?" She ran to me, and I didn't have to worry about hiding how upset I'd been. I was just thrilled to have her back.

If her adventure meant anything, perhaps she was letting me know that she could leave if she wanted to and that staying was her choice. Then again, maybe it was just something crazy to do. I don't know, and Maggie isn't telling.

We're out the door, with no time for Maggie to get too warm, for it is seriously warming up out here. We'll have to leave her at home now. See, the staff people behind the desk at the vet's office just now were not doing much. If I had time on my hands, I might be tempted to hang over the counter and shoot the breeze. Deadly.

Let's get Maggie home, and we'll pack a lunch and make callbacks. It's almost 10:00, a time when established clients know they have a good chance of catching me at home. Answering the phone and doing callbacks are best done standing over the appointment book. The slow creep of high tech may excite some people. I just see more possibilities for distraction and error, so I will resist new gadgets until I can honestly see their benefit. Besides, I hate spending money. Small businesses should keep overhead as low as possible. The exception is advertising. I will spend money on promo and do without groceries. Hey, Coke and Pepsi advertise, right? And there's not a person in this world who doesn't know those brands. So, yes, I'm willing to advertise, and really happy to learn of new places to do so. I'll build my little empire one dog walk at a time.

I have to watch this – end of a school zone and we may have Barney Fife in his cruiser behind the shrubbery over there. Small town hazard. The best strategy I have found for how to behave when the cops see me going a little over the limit is to look them right in the eye, smile, and give them a big Miss America wave. That's right. Act like you're so glad to see them. Cops have a thankless job.

And a last word on promo. I mentioned earlier how Poppy the parakeet learned to make the sounds of his human as she conversed from another room. I called it "inadvertent training." I inadvertently trained the entire staff of a veterinary clinic to have reduced expectations – well, let me start at the beginning. Quarterly, I take treats to all the groomers and vets in the area. Everyone gets a big barrel of pretzels or animal crackers, with my biz card attached to the lid. The groomers and vets who have sent me new clients during that quarter don't get pretzels, but rather a box of the best chocolates I can afford. I always thought I was pretty clever, what with building in an incentive and all. Then one day, a receptionist in a small vet clinic introduced me to a new employee as "the pretzel lady." Oops. They had never sent me a new client, which would have been the only way they could have known about my two-tiered reward system. So, of course, I had to give everyone chocolates the next time around, explaining that if they liked them, referrals could keep the good stuff coming.

Well, the old place is still standing. "Hey, Maggie, jump out. You're home now until evening." Yes, I talk to her all the time. She knows only about 30-40 words, but I want to believe that my speech conveys meaningful intent or emotion. We've spent long periods of time together when I didn't say anything, and she was just fine. It would seem that I have a need to speak, but she doesn't have a need to hear it.

First, let me get the phone. It's always easier and just plain better to talk to the caller. "Hello…yes, hi, Betsy. Wow, that's coming right up. How is that rascal? ….Oh, good. Well, that's often the problem when they're peeing just outside the pan.….Right, something wrong with the pan, or the litter, and you were keeping it clean....I'm glad she likes the new litter.... Sure, just give me the exact dates. Okay, and are you including Monday morning? Or do you plan to feed her before you leave? ... You're a wise woman. I'll be there around 9:00 the first day, and see the kitty each day at about that time. I'll be looking for your check – that's your reservation, and I look forward to seeing your lovable fur factory. Thanks for asking me to take care of her."

So many people think they'll have time to feed their pets before they leave in the morning for the airport. I sometimes show up the next day to find desperately hungry animals. We're just too rushed when we're trying to get out the door.

Let me put a tickler on the day she wants me to start. I'll change that to visits in the appointment book when the check comes. The tickler reminds me to follow up if the check doesn't come. Yes, that happens, too. I could just assume that the owners made other plans, but that has never happened. In every instance, they just forgot to send the check. I feel responsible to follow through, for myself, the pets, and the reputation of my business. I make a note of the call, too, when it came in, and what we said. When I write in the individual visits, I put a green dot on the first visit and a red dot on the last. Why? I caught myself once, stopping that recording process to take a call. A "last" visit was in the book, but it was merely where I had stopped writing. Yep. Good thing I realized it. That's why the red dot matters. At times, I have checked obsessively the record of dates discussed against the visits written in the book.

Well, I'm hungry. Let's have a second go at that blackberry pie. Anyone will tell you I love the animals, but life without pie would have questionable value. This ritual is called Second Breakfast.

Let's try this number. Voice mail, I guess. "Hello, this is Diana Carter, the pet sitter. You called about boarding, and that isn't really pet sitting. It's kenneling, and I don't do that. I pamper animals in their own homes. Call back if you'd like to hear about good kennels in your area, or if you'd like to discuss the benefits of pet sitting for your pets. Thanks for your interest in the service."

I sometimes wonder if I say all that in my sleep. Let's try this one.

"Hi, is this Ron? This is Diana Carter, the pet sitter. Right, you called about the Rottie. Tell me about your dog…. Okay….I see. No, the care would be in your own home…. Before you go on, let me just say that I would need to test the dog's level of sociability first…. Yes, I do take care of Rottweilers, but they've always been dogs I knew as puppies. I know the owners, and that they invest time and effort in their pets' training and socialization…. What's that? …Yours doesn't like to be trained? Uh-huh… have you thought about kenneling him with your vet? I mean, they know him there…Oh, dear. They won't take him at all? Oh, my…everyone, huh? So, you're desperate. I appreciate the call, but I'm not the answer to your problem….Well, the dog isn't the problem, either. Yes… good luck to you. Bye."

I feel sorry for the dog. What will happen to him? He's managed to bite every staff person at the vet's office.

Chances are he wasn't born that way, and I doubt that he'll enjoy a long, happy life.

Now that's an extreme case, but I don't take every job. Not every dog does well at home alone. It depends on socialization, training, and life experience. Typically, the most anxious dogs are likely to be the retreads. There's a world of difference between a dog lovingly raised and trained within one family and a dog who "lost" his first family. I don't know one word that covers loss, surrender, confiscation, carelessness, dumping, and any other event or circumstance that may separate a dog from his first human family. Dogs have minds and emotions. They are not statuary, nor are they meant to be pawns in foolish human politics.

And the mistreated among them never forget, for the rest of their lives, that human beings are capable of abuse, neglect, betrayal, disloyalty, and all other manner of heartbreaking behaviors. If any dog is going to have a destructive anxiety attack when left alone – and this includes the ones adopted into very conscientious families – it's likely to be a dog that has been re-adopted.

If a dog you are considering will not be the subject of your loving attention forever, you must not adopt him. Get a figurine if you like the look of a dog around the house, but can't invest time with him every day.

My sweet Maggie has a calm and a dignity that I have not observed in a rescued dog. She is not anxious or insecure. She is strong, self-assured, and joyful. She doesn't chew anything but her own toys. Maggie is my companion and she knows it. "Retread" dogs, in the right hands, can blossom, but there will always be a shadow of doubt in those big brown eyes. Many will never be fully trustworthy home alone. They simply know too much about us to relax. We have given them cause for worry.

Well, on the somewhat lighter subject of my baking, this pie crust is one of my best. I don't know why the quality varies so much from one pie to the next, since I never use any other recipe. Oh, well, I'd eat it anyway, flaky or tough. I'm a barbarian.

"Hey, Maggie, want this last piece of crust?" Yep, that's what I do. I always give her the last piece of whatever I'm eating. If a client did that in front of me with a dog, I'd be tempted to deliver a righteous sermon about all the reasons it's wrong. Terrible habit, and I wouldn't recommend it. I vaguely remember when I started doing that. The result is that all the while I'm eating, I have a pair of intent brown eyes on me. It's okay. We're pals and we share everything. She's active enough to stay slim. It seems that most Labs get fat, and that's because they always seem hungry. Their humans cave and feed them all the time. Eek!

"Call incoming, or I'm hearing bells. Hello? Yes, it is.... Oh, my. No, I don't take care of lizards...Well, they aren't quite domesticated animals...Yes, I'm sure it is exciting.... Yes, and they're beautiful. Most animals are. I'm sorry, but I draw the line at caged birds. I do take care of them, but lizards – what's that? Iguanas? Yes, I consider them lizards, and I did take care of an iguana once. He was part of a menagerie that included three cats and a dog. He lived in a huge glass case, and over three days I had to have very little to do with him. Just for the record, I wouldn't take that job again…..No, I'm going to have to decline. I wish I could help, but I don't know of anyone else you might call…. Thanks for calling, and good luck."

Yes, I said too much, and that happens when I'm annoyed. I don't like being pressured, and I have a problem with taking on exotics. Our track record with domesticated animals is so poor that we have no business taking on other species. So, no, I am not an animal "nut." I have standards, and I don't take every job.

Okay, what's in the fridge for lunch? I have to pack something for the road. Ooh, slices of cheddar cheese and this very ripe tomato with some good bread. Then something for crunch. Baby carrots, of course.

"Maggie, you're in the 'uh-oh' zone." Isn't that wonderful? She walks right out of the kitchen. No dog wants to hear "uh-oh." She already knows she doesn't belong in here when I'm preparing food. "Love you, darlin' girl." Another dog might sit in the dining room, waiting for a treat. We both know there won't be one, so she heads for the couch. Refill water bottle, got the sandwich, and everything else is already in the car.

Another phone call. This is a truly good day.

"Hello? …Yes, it is…. I certainly do. I've known them a long time. How nice of them to give you my number…. Sure, let me tell you how it works. I take care of pets in their own homes on a long or short term basis. The standard of care is based on wanting the pets to have a stress-free time while their family is gone. I feed and exercise your pets according to their usual schedule....the number of visits per day would be up to you, whatever you think they need...sure, three is typical for dogs. I am insured and bonded, and can give you references. Tell me about your pets....I see...a Lab – ah, six years old...and a calico.. eighteen? Good for you. You seem tentative... aha – the medication isn't a problem. Yes, I can give meds. If you're going away in a week, we should meet as soon as possible. Not to pressure you, but both you and your pets have to like me and trust me. If any part of this doesn't work out, you'll need time to make other arrangements.... yes, tomorrow afternoon could work. Which is better, 2:00 or 3:00? .....okay. Yes, we'll complete a service agreement together so there's a written understanding of what you want me to do. The address?... Fine. I know the area.....and the best phone number? ....Okay, and I'll want time to walk your dog while I'm there, just to make sure he's manageable. .... I agree, Labs are great, my favorite breed. I also think they're puppies until they're middle aged! ...good, I'm glad to know that. All dogs should go through obedience...and I like what it says about you. You must be very caring and conscientious. Well, fine, I look forward to meeting you and your pets. Bye now."

That went well. Two perfectly spoiled pets, and the dog has actually gone through obedience. Sent to me by long-time clients. Those lovin' sweeties have Godiva chocolates and a free dog walk in their future if this works out.

"Bye, Mag. Take care of the kitties. Here – a hug. Hugga-wugga-wugga. Ooh, yes, I love you, too. Go hold down the couch until I get back." Oh, and there's that happy puppy sound.

We'll get out of here before the phone rings again. I do prefer catching the calls as they come in, but we need to hit the road.

Jumping into the car without Maggie always feels lonely. It's over 70 degrees now, so she'll eventually migrate from the couch to the kitchen floor. She loves the car, but it holds no novelty for her, and she has learned that a warm day means a day at home.

We're off to Sheffield. It's a bit of a trek, but this was one of my first jobs. I spend a half hour playing with two beautiful Dobermans. There have been moments when I've thought, "This is a day I will remember forever." I strongly feel that if I live to be one hundred, I'll remember the dogs we're about to visit. I don't know why I haven't had the urge to go out and adopt a Dobie, but that hasn't happened yet. Sweet, strong, beautiful and protective. What's not to love?

CHAPTER 5

11:00am Growing a Spine

So why would anyone want to be a pet sitter? I work every day of the year, and holidays most of all. Friends who want to see me have to schedule something well in advance, and I have at times cancelled fun with friends because of work. The work comes first. I take care of the business, and the business takes care of me. I've learned the hard way that loyalty to my livelihood cannot falter.

I started this business when I was desperate. One morning, after trying for a time to make a living selling real estate, I was in jeopardy of losing everything. I used to refer to that time as "the troubles," but now I call it my midlife trifecta. I was in the wrong line of work, in a bad marriage, and going through menopause. The overall feeling was adolescence redux. The mantra is this : "I have the worst life ever, and it will never get better, and no could possibly understand." There were procedural and legal remedies for the first two problems. For menopause? Well, there's an old Pink Floyd song with the line, "There's someone in my head but it's not me." Yes, it felt that strange.

Overwhelmed as I was, I was still me. I came fighting to the top of that mostly self-made mess, and managed to get my life straightened around. I mentioned earlier that I was selling real estate. Before that, I had been a social worker in blind rehab, and loved it. Social work was what I was born to do. I loved the work that helped make people stronger and more able to cope with life's challenges. My friends were social workers, too, and we often talked about the day when we might have to leave the work we cared about. We wanted to earn what one of us called "grown-up" wages. As I recall, one of my friends went off to become an event planner, and tripled her income almost immediately. I began selling real estate, an easy business to get into, with no startup capital necessary. Big mistake. It wasn't long before those anemic social work paychecks would have looked pretty good. I spent too much time in that real estate office, telling myself, "This has to work out." I'll spare you the details, but suffice it to say that one of my flaws is staying with failing projects too long.

One morning at about 8:30, looking like Real Estate Lady from head to toe and heading out to the weekly staff meeting, something about the desk in my dining room caught my attention. Beside the basket of bills I couldn't pay, there were writing projects, sewing projects and garden plans pushed to the side. So many things I cared about were languishing because of my new-found poverty. At my core, I needed to do something useful and to be in regular contact with people who cared about the same things I did. In an immediate sense, I needed money. Enough for groceries and a tank of gas would have been glorious.

I sat down at the desk and pulled out a yellow note pad. Remembering the words of a motivational speaker, I wrote down all the things I cared about. Not the little things, but things I could, in that speaker's words, "give my life to." My list was animals, gardening, writing, and sewing. The next step was to look at those categories and identify a need. That was easier than I thought it would be. I had heard people say that they couldn't travel as freely as they wanted to because they had no one to take care of their pets. I had said it myself. I believe I've mentioned that a friend of mine did me that "favor" a few years earlier, throwing food and water at my cats for five days. I didn't stop to wonder whether this was something I could do for a living or whether this could be a viable business. I gave birth right then and there to something I didn't know was in me.

You must understand that I had never heard of pet sitting as a business, but rather I was re-inventing the wheel. Having had pets all my life, I had a good idea of what dogs and cats might need from a care provider. I came up with a list of services and accompanying fees, and then I typed up a flyer. With the Yellow Pages propped on my knees, I created a list of all the places I might want to drop off copies and multiplied that by twenty. I would have to live on soup for a week, but having those flyers printed and distributed was suddenly all I cared about. I was excited for the first time in a long time. I glanced at the clock, and realized I had dreamed up this scheme complete with details in under three hours. I don't exercise the gift of foresight very well, but something made me write down the time. I had sat down at 8:30 and it was now 11:15. Staff meeting? Oops. The telling thing was I didn't care. My new project was all-important.

Real traction came from the monthly newsletter, in which I wrote a little about the business in general, opinion pieces about pet care issues, pet profiles, and book reviews. Vets and groomers started sending me business, because, as I was told repeatedly, the newsletter reflected some knowledge of and devotion to pet care. The first few pets I took care of, not surprisingly, were recovering from surgeries of different kinds, some having taken ill just before a planned family vacation. That people took a leap of faith and entrusted me with their recovering pets was mind-boggling. They had to be going on whatever their vets were saying, for I could offer no references at first.

Three things came from that experience. Those early clients graciously gave me the glowing references that they had had to do without. I gained additional experience with medicating and with bathing the sutures of pets, some of whom were in no mood to be trifled with. My reflexes became faster and my pain endurance improved along the way. The most profound development was that I began to feel proud, competent, trustworthy, and strong. I had lost touch with those traits in myself, and now I felt whole again.

Other aspects of my business were shaped in part by friends I made along the way. Those early clients and a few groomers kept telling me I wasn't charging enough for services. One day, tired of hearing that piece of advice, I tripled my rates and waited for the world to end. No one noticed! If anything, business got better. I was learning whom to listen to, and the listening and the learning were far from over.

Most important, one person taught me how to stand up for myself. You should be so lucky, to have someone appear, almost out of the blue, who will raise you up to a place you didn't even know you needed to be.

I met Frank when my business had been struggling along for about a year or so. I needed a part-time job with flexible hours, something I could schedule around the morning kitty visits and the noonday dog walks. Frank had been selling antique and collectible toys for many years, and I went to work for him on a very part-time basis, handling mail order for him when he was away doing toy shows. The only time this work was actually any fun was when Frank was home and I would take Maggie with me to his place to box up orders. Maggie rarely saw men and seemed fascinated by them. She actually worshipped Frank. To his great amusement, she would exhaust herself bowing repeatedly to him. She could be a real embarrassment.

Much more fun and stimulating was working Frank's small store one or two days a week. It was ultimately the site of a great life lesson. Here was the set-up.

I got to know Frank's regular customers, people who came in nearly every Saturday to look over the inventory of toys. They were mostly middle-aged men, hoping to get back in touch with some childhood memory. Every once in a while some Disney employee would stop by, and even toy designers. I built up the business, letting Frank know what collectors were asking for, and he would get the toys to me. Some of the best customers after a while were people who had never actually met Frank, since he was usually traveling.

When shoppers questioned Frank's pricing, I always shrugged and told them to talk to him when he was around. I honestly knew nothing about the business myself, and had only a small amount of leeway in bargaining. All members of the public were potential buyers and sellers, so basic courtesy was in order.

As I think about it now, that seems reasonable, but human behavior - news flash - isn't always based on reason. One weekend, Frank was in town and came into the store to catch up on things. It wasn't long before he was engaged in a conversation with some of the regulars. They had been looking forward to meeting him, and he and they were enjoying some incomprehensible guy-bonding nonsense. I busied myself with other customers and putting up inventory.

One of the men was looking at some action figures. He looked right into Frank's face and told him that the prices were inflated. Frank didn't miss a beat, saying, "If you can't afford it, maybe you need a better job."

My head snapped around. He surely wasn't being rude to people who spent money on this stuff every week. The customer's faced reddened. He said, "You're one thin-skinned son of a pup." Frank bent his large 6'2" frame toward the man, who was much shorter. "And you need to understand that I make my living in this market. I deal in this stuff every day of my life. People who do business with me know me as knowledgeable, honest, and fair. I know what I'm doin', pal, and you can take it or leave it."

I was devastated, as I watched the man and his friends walking away. "Frank, that's one of your best customers, even though you never met him before. And now we'll never see him again."

Frank laughed. "I promise you he'll be back. In fact, I'll bet you he'll be back in about fifteen minutes."

I looked at him, puzzled.

"He has to lick his wounds, cuss me out, get a little support from his friends, then consider how badly he wants to make the buy. Fifteen minutes." Not only did the man come back, he bought the item he wanted, and his friends made purchases, too. I shook my head. Male hoo-doo, I thought.

Over coffee, Frank straightened me out. He didn't couch his remarks in the context of my working for him, but in working for myself. "Diana, you have to change the way you deal with people. You're too nice, and annoyingly self-effacing. People like you, and that counts for something, but it isn't everything. Start with this – you know more than the average person about pet care. Learn to flaunt it, short of being obnoxious." He gave me that devilish, maddening grin, then he gave me a headful of advice.

I jotted down everything he told me, that day and throughout the short time I knew him. Here's the list.

- Be sure people know you are truthful and trustworthy

- Figure out what your costs are and charge what you're worth

- Stand your ground on fees and policies; explain but don't over-explain

- If they can't afford you, that's their problem - don't lower prices or give discounts just to make people happy.

- Experience will teach you where your weak spots are. Learn from mistakes and don't let those "dogs" bite you twice

- Build good will by making realistic promises, then over-deliver

- Business comes before friendship. Stick to core principles and practices. People must respect you. If your clients like you and become friends, that's a bonus, never a primary goal

- Be humble. Ask the seasoned professionals in related fields for advice, and then listen.

I saved the best for last. I couldn't soften the language on these last two items. Here's Frank's wisdom in his own words.

"When times get tough, get meaner than a junkyard dog." That means facing a slump by slapping on a smile and running around to vets' and groomers' offices with boxes of chocolates and a fistful of business cards. Skip groceries (yours, not your pets') if you have to, to give the very best you can afford. Don't spend any time crying. Get busy. Get creative. Tell everybody that business is great. Mean it.

"Don't take crap from anybody, not ever." That sounds simple, but it's the biggest lesson of all. I have since given the same advice to many people. Here's how I express it: honor your own life. People speak carelessly and sometimes hurtfully, mainly because they can. I have learned to ignore it. I turn down potential clients who are disrespectful. My first responsibility is to honor the life God gave me.

Working Frank's toy business on my own, I began to practice the script he had taught me. I treated Frank's customers as he did, eventually with his same self-assurance and success. I had the same positive results, time after time. (Actually, I had been told the same things in the real estate biz, but I never had a chance to see how it worked). I then began standing up for my own pricing and practices in the pet sitting business. I asserted what I knew about pet care, and people respected what I had to say.

Frank's advice was meant to help me succeed in my one-woman business, and it worked better than I could have imagined. To my amazement, I began to feel differently about myself. The best measurement for how much I changed over time was any encounter I had with people who had known me before. I thought I was still the same old me with a few changes, but no. I was now relating to people very differently. For example, I had a call from a woman who had known me during the brief time that I was selling real estate. She gushed over the fact that I was now pet sitting, because she had two large rare-breed dogs that needed daily walks.

She expressed confidence that I would do a good job. I was interested, but not for long. When I told her what I charged, she immediately asked me how much of a discount I was willing to offer. My answer was, "None." "Why? You know me," she said incredulously, "I'm a nice person. Besides, I have two dogs, and this would be an ongoing job for you. You can surely afford to give me a discount." I explained that none of my creditors gave me discounts, so I didn't offer them either.

This was someone who, with her husband, had taken up a lot of my time a few years earlier, demanding to see pricey historic homes all over northeast Ohio. If they ever bought anything, it wasn't from me. They ran me around for weeks, and I just kept driving on empty and smiling through my tears. I was a well-trained doormat who was destined never to make a living in that industry.

Now this same woman was on the phone, beginning to wonder who she was talking to. She began to sound tense, saying slowly, "You aren't the way I remember. You were always so –"

"Compliant? Yes, I remember. If that's the Diana you're looking for, she doesn't live in this body anymore. You say you love your dogs and would do anything for them. At the same time, you want discounted care. Call me when you stop contradicting yourself. Goodbye now." I didn't expect her to call back, didn't want her to, and she never did. She was, once again, looking for someone to push around. I found the experience of pushing back exhilarating. Through that and similar exchanges, I realized both the extent to which I had always been pushed around, and how much I had changed.

Until I met Frank, I always thought I was supposed to be nice to people and to worry about what people thought of me. It had never occurred to me that other people didn't seem to operate that way, not even in the hardest times of my life. Now I saw it. All I would now require from others, as well as from myself, was respect. This may sound elementary to some, but it goes against the way I was brought up. I had now come to see the world through a different lens. This eventually carried over into social and familial relationships as well. Anyone who knew me before I knew Frank was taken aback. I continued to get a lot of "Wow, what happened to you?" when people found they couldn't walk all over me. I was no longer a door mat, and anyone who couldn't accept that got left in a cloud of dust.

My business would never have succeeded if I had not developed a spine. Thank you, Frank, wherever you are.

CHAPTER 6

11:30am Beautiful Dobies

Okay, we're almost there and it's just about 11:30. As for why I became a pet sitter, I grew up with animals. Cats and I always seem to understand each other. Dogs generally do not bark at me. I can't explain it, but there it is. My life is good with animals in it. I recognized a need in the marketplace when I tried that twenty-nine cent test. Many people in my circle of acquaintances wanted in-home pet care, and no one was offering it. I wanted to go into a business that made sense for me. I know who I am when I'm working, and this business requires me to work every day of the year. I meet marvelous people and lots of perfectly spoiled pets. Why would I want to do anything else?

Speaking of which, here's our stop. I get a kick out of looking up and seeing those two Dobie faces peering at me from under the lace curtains. Samson and Zoey – a study in contrast. Samson's ears stand up as you might expect to see in a Doberman. Surprisingly, his tail is not docked. I understood the practice of docking the first time he wagged his tail fiercely and hit the backs of my legs with that long whip-like tail. I nearly fell over from the pain. His family found him as a starving puppy in a public park. He has been a rather thin fellow ever since, but not for lack of good food.

Zoey came from the breeder with a docked tail, but her adoptive family opted for the uncropped ears. Her floppy ears give her a sweet look, but don't be fooled. She is a smart, gentle friend who happens to have a dead serious streak. Yep, she's all Dobie.

"Hey, kids! Oh, Zoey, yes, you are a sweetie. Yes, I'm glad to see you, too. Now stay off. Good girl. Come here, Sammy. Since when are you so shy? There, let's get a proper ear scratching. You are a soulful boy. Go out? You bet!"

We'll spend a high-quality half hour mostly tossing a tennis ball. Straight out through the patio doors they have a dog run. Samson will catch a ball over and over again as if he's never done it before. Zoey always lies down, out of the way, watching with interest but never participating. She stretches, ruminates, and gathers the warmth of the sunshine into her fur. Being a beautiful presence is typically all she offers in my time with her. She is a true princess.

In the dim long ago, someone discovered that dogs love tennis balls. Let us all be grateful for the joy that knowledge has brought to the world. "C'mon, Sammy, let's go." I toss the ball so it has a high but short arc. We have to stay inside the chain link run. After all, I'm the one who has to fetch if I overshoot the fence. A couple of warm-ups. "Good boy. Zoey, doesn't this look like fun?" Clearly not. She's just like my own Maggie, not interested in the least in physical exertion. For Samson's part, he deserves a good pitcher, and I do not have a good arm. He catches like nobody's business. Sometimes that big dog is wonderfully close to taking flight, and it's quite a sight to behold. Let's see if I can get this one high enough – here we go. And there he goes. Up, up, turning slightly and stretching completely out to catch the ball, turning again, almost defying gravity, and turning once more before he comes down. Samson lands with the same grace that carried him skyward. On that second turn there's a sweet spot where I'm sure he'll sprout wings and keep going. I'm glad he doesn't. I'd really miss him. "Feels good, hey, Sammy? Yes, that's a good boy." That sun is unrelentingly warm, there's no shade here, and black fur heats up fast. "Let's go in, guys."

They'll get water if they want it, and I'll settle here on the family room floor. Zoey and I share some time together, while Samson cools down. "Hey, Zoey, come see me." I don't need to watch the time, because she knows when a half hour is up, and will escort me to the door. "That's right. Come lie down here beside me. Every princess needs a tummy rub once in a while." The simple act of showing her belly, to demonstrate trust, always stops me for a moment. So it is with any animal that trusts me. I don't take that for granted; in fact, I strive to earn that trust with every contact. Working with animals every day keeps my awareness keen that I'm The Other. I belong to a dangerous species, and the animals, never mind the tail wagging and the purring, are well aware. All I can do is try to be worthy.

This sweet-faced Doberman was ferocious one day when a man and woman came to the door, wanting me to open the storm door so they could pass a pamphlet to me. I reached forward to lock the storm door, and Zoey, perhaps misunderstanding my intention, nearly knocked me out of the way. I smiled and said, "I don't think the dogs will let us talk." The woman looked first at Zoey in full "lunge-any-second-now" mode and then Samson, who was adopting a similar stance (always the follower!). Surprisingly, she said, "Can't you control your dogs?" I smiled. "Oh, yes. Don't you see they're contained? Have a good day."

I felt so safe. I don't know what they actually wanted, but Zoey wasn't buying it. Her judgement was good enough for me.

On a beautiful country property a couple of years ago, I was taking care of two Shar-peis. That's another breed I always approach with respect. As with Samson and Zoey, the female seemed to be the male's tutor. All the homes on that stretch of road were newer, with new construction going in all around. This was a Saturday morning, and I was just about to leave. An authoritatively loud knock on the front door startled all of us. The female Shar-pei went into attack mode. Her reaction worried me. Now, I don't open any door without knowing who's out there, but her behavior put me on guard.

When I looked out the front window, I saw a pleasant-looking gray-haired man in jeans and a white tee shirt, holding a clipboard under his arm. A white unmarked van was parked in front of the house. I thought he might be a contractor or repairman, so through the closed window I asked him who he was looking for. Now the game was in play.

He did that funny thing some people do when they can't believe they're being questioned. He looked away, blinked, and looked back at me. "I'm looking for the owner of the property."

"Okay, what name do you have there?"

"Where?"

"Right there – on your clipboard. What name is on your paperwork? "

The man blew his cheeks out a little. "I need to get into the house."

"Tell me who you're looking for, so I can tell you if you have the right house."

"Look, lady. I'm from the title company, and there's a problem with the way the paperwork was done on the sale of this house."

"Well, that is interesting. I know a few things about that title company, and I know that all your title company's employees drive marked cars. I also know that, even if the Vatican were transferring title, it simply wouldn't happen between Friday evening and Monday morning. I don't know who you are, but I'll let the police know you were here. Now please go away."

The man gave me a long, dirty look before walking back to his vehicle. I was only sorry that he couldn't see two Shar-peis digging their back feet into the carpeting, getting spring-loaded for a jump at his throat.

It occurred to me that I had read a few newspaper accounts over the years about women who were murdered in their own homes. These murders happened during the day, and there was no sign of forced entry. I felt a chill. Knowing how some women try to avoid unpleasantness and don't ask enough questions, I saw how a jerk like that could bully someone and gain access to a residence where he didn't belong. My heart seemed to pump faster for quite a while. I had to go back that evening! What if he broke into the house? Oh, wait. I laughed to myself. The dogs would finish him off.

"What is it, Zoey? Oh, sure, time for me to go. Okay. I hate to leave you." And I really do. This house is airy, sun-washed and peaceful. I love the dogs and the people who live here, and I hope their lives are as happy as this atmosphere suggests.

"Goodbye, Zoey. Goodbye, Samson. I'll see you tomorrow. I love you." And I truly do.

Now for a change of pace. The two gorgeous horses we're going to see are tended by a woman who knows her stuff, but most of the other horse owners in this area have relocated. Her horses are calm and happy, living in a nearly spotless barn, with easy access to beautiful pasture. They live in Avon, a community that was a sleepy and charming rural community up until some developers fell in love with the idea of transforming it a few short years ago. Now it's rapidly becoming something else. The lady and her horses are a relic of the passing era. The loosely organized culture of horse enthusiasts has shifted geographically to still-rural areas. Those people are quite often old friends who have known each other since they were 4-H'ers, and they pitch in to take care of each other's horses. This client is now isolated, and sometimes must do what people who are new to horse ownership often do – she calls a pet sitter.

Before we get there, I want to say something more about dogs and their ability to judge people. We can learn from them, perhaps because they aren't blinded by some of the props that often distract us. One of my favorite dogs is a Keeshond named Nikki. What a great breed! I've known a number of Keeshonds, and their humans usually see them as bubbleheads. Keeshonds are actually smart and highly trainable, but their sweet, playful nature makes them seem otherwise. Nikki would not be quieted one day when her human, a single woman, stood talking to the appliance repairman. He was there to look at the washing machine, and Nikki's human thought he was kind of cute. She later described him to me as tall, trim and blond. He had a fresh haircut , and – I know this was important to her – he wore a very nice watch. She told me about this because Nikki behaved so unusually. A Keeshond will typically let the world know when a stranger approaches, but Nikki growled, barked and paced the entire time the guy was there. Her human was ready to throw her out. The woman's question to me was, "What's wrong with her? You know Nikki. Have you ever seen her act this way?"

"No, but I would trust Nikki. Is he coming back, or is the work done?"

"Ha! He didn't finish the work, but I don't know why. Maybe we spent too much time talking. The really weird part is that a second fella came out a few days later, and he and Nikki were instant friends. You should have seen him. Shaggy hair and he needed a shave. He didn't smell very fresh either. I couldn't wait to get him out of the house. He did a good job, hugged Nikki goodbye, and was out the door. What's wrong with her?"

Well, you must know what I said. You know as well as I do that dogs don't care about watches, haircuts, or – goodness knows – when anybody had a bath last. They can smell adrenaline on us. They can sense intent. Shoot, maybe they can smell a guilty conscience. I don't know. In any case, I trust Nikki's judgement. If your dog growls at someone, pay attention. Yes, I say this as someone whose own dog only barks at bees (Maggie was stung on the nose as a puppy), but I have a little experience with the canine nature.

If you have a rescue dog, his judgement may be one of the aspects of his canine psyche that wasn't properly cared for in his earlier life. While waiting with a very nervous kitty at the vet's office several years ago, I saw a young man walk in cautiously with a large mixed breed dog. Satisfied after looking over the half dozen people in the small waiting room, he took a seat and put his dog in a sit-stay. The small waiting room was conducive to conversation, and an older woman asked the young man about the dog's breed background. German shepherd mix? The young man was a bit shy at first, but then said he really didn't know. He had adopted the dog from a local animal shelter about a year earlier, and they had become friends right away. He began to go on about how friendly and trainable the dog was. I was still a social worker at the time, so I had a heightened sense of the oncoming "however."

The young man said of the handsome, relaxed dog that now lay at his feet, "Sometimes he goes completely insane. It can be scary." "How so?" the woman asked. The young man said that his dog hated men of a particular description. "Old white men wearing clodhopper boots, overalls and ball caps infuriate him. You know those geezers with the loud voices. " We all laughed. Some of us nodded with understanding.

I am so glad that I've lived long enough that I don't have to make anything up.

Over the next several minutes, a few people with pets left and a few more arrived. Then the door opened and a man walked in alone. Those of us who had heard the young man's comments sat up a little straighter. The newcomer was an old man wearing mud-covered heavy boots, overalls, and a greasy old engineer's cap.

The young man murmured something comforting to the dog, as the dog sniffed the air and stirred. The old man approached the receptionist's desk and spoke in a very loud voice, inquiring about the status of an animal that had had surgery. The dog jumped to his feet and went into a seething fury. The young man was holding him by the collar, but the dog clearly wanted a piece of the old man. It was indeed scary. My head bumped the wall behind me. The dog's teeth were bared, and his fur stood up in a ridge along his spine. Even the fur on his tail bushed out. The old man interrupted himself once to look back at the dog, and then went on haranguing the receptionist. Eventually he left. The dog lay down at his human's feet, exhausted.

That dog had learned to hate people that fit a very narrow profile. I have wondered ever since whether he would be able to pass judgement accurately on anyone, as I have seen so many dogs do.

CHAPTER 7

12:15pm Blond Chestnuts

I have to slow down here, because the house and barn we're looking for are somewhat obscured by these big trees. Okay, here we are. We'll make sure these beauties have plenty of fresh water and some hay. I do exactly as their human instructs, because I don't know the first thing about horses.

"Hey, guys. What's happening in equine land?" I have described these two to a friend, who tells me they are probably blond chestnuts. Their human didn't say, but they are stunning, with tannish bodies and cream-colored manes and tails.

"What an eyeful you both are. Oh, yes, my dears, you are so pretty."

They always look at each other before coming slowly toward me. Their stalls are open so they can go out the back doors to the pasture whenever they want to, but I can count on their greeting me. The horses already know that I am equinophobic, even though I make a conscious effort to modulate my breathing and my movements. There is no fooling a horse. These two clever characters like to double team me. Sugar seems eager to take a little hay from my hand, while Mischief —rightly named- sneaks around to the back and tugs on my back pocket. I manage not to scream, but let out a "Hey!" They share so many glances while toying with me that they appear telepathic. They sniff my hair and gently shove me around until I say firmly, "That's enough."

Mischief is the larger one, and I assume a male. Yes, I'd know if I were to look, but I'm busy regulating my breathing. He could knock me down and crush me if he wanted to. He won't, because I wouldn't be any fun anymore. I consider this part of my education. I figure that with enough exposure to horses, I'll be able to lose the fear, and just admire them for their powerful beauty and great spirit. We'll see.

Okay, they're already bored with me. Maybe someday I'll come and they'll greet me with something like a feline treatment, looking disdainful and then ignoring me altogether. That just may happen when they find they can no longer make my heart race. I can only hope. For now, they're sauntering out to the pasture. Once there, I won't see them again. I can tend to my duties without being nibbled at. I'll rinse out these water buckets and refill them. What a classy barn! Hot and cold running water. They both get some hay in their impeccable stalls, even though they have some good pasture out there. As I go out, let me double check to see that all doors and gates are latched. The human in charge understands very well how smart these horses are, for the latches all have multiple-step mechanisms that I initially found challenging.

I once took care of a horse that was so difficult the owners had set up an elaborate pulley system for changing the water buckets. They warned me not to get too close, although I had to get close enough to toss in fresh hay. One day I did get close and didn't move back fast enough. She tossed the hay right back at me, and it landed on top of my head. I was shaking hay seeds out of my hair all day. That is sometimes the situation, though, with people calling pet sitters to take care of horses. They may be city people new to the country, and don't yet have those connections in the horse culture. The related problem is that, as city folk, they were sold a horse that a more knowledgeable person wouldn't want.

Let me just take a look around outside. My lovely tormentors may give me a hard time, but I'm responsible for them. Don't misunderstand me. I'm afraid of them, but that doesn't keep me from respecting and admiring them. I count them among my teachers. So let's take a peek. It would be my luck that, if I didn't check, a section of fence would have fallen down. Nope, all is well. Time to head out. "You kids be good. Stay beautiful. I'll see you again." Yes, I always say goodbye.

My stomach says it's time for apple slices. Too bad I just have carrots. Oh, yes, and that messy cheese and tomato sandwich. I'll work on that at the red lights. Here we go, heading back to Oberlin.

Maggie should have the chance to come here someday. Unlike me, she has no fear of horses. She appears to worship them. She met two horses last winter when I was taking her for a short walk. Next to a country home where I had been taking care of a cat, a large black male horse and a smaller brown mare were standing in a snowy pasture. Maggie pulled me toward the fence. The mare seemed to be curious about us and came up to the fence. When Maggie reached her, the mare gently dropped her head to Maggie's level. Maggie began to bow. This was a solemn act, not like the playful bowing she and I do all the time. She bowed repeatedly, and only stopped when the mare made a gentle head movement and an almost inaudible sound. All of this meant something to both animals. Maggie approached her with tail wagging rapidly, and they nuzzled each other through the fence.

The mare whinnied at the male and made a "come here" motion with her head. When he looked away, she gently stomped her hoof. He looked back at the mare, then at Maggie. He came over, waited for Maggie to stop bowing at him, and then nuzzled her for a moment. It was all perfunctory for him. He just wanted to please the mare. He turned and walked away. Maggie began bowing again. Eventually the mare tired of the adoration and wandered off.

Horses are certainly astonishing creatures. What I witnessed on that snowy morning did not involve me at all. In fact, Maggie and the horses didn't seem aware of me. In any case, I suspect Maggie's communing with the horses in that pasture meant far more than I will ever understand.

We'll drop down 301 South on the east side of Elyria. This route takes me close to some pets I haven't seen for a while. To the east, I used to walk a very large dog, whose breed I cannot mention. Almost any modifier would identify the family, and I don't want to do that. I quit working for them because they clearly had the dog for status only. After two years of suggesting, cajoling, begging, and preaching, I announced that I was through. My business was growing, and I didn't want to be associated with a situation where the pet was mistreated. The neglect and abuse could be interpreted as well-intentioned foolishness, as the owner gleefully pointed out. I couldn't prove a thing, so I walked out on a steady job. The dog was adorable, and I was helpless to alter the situation. I hoped that when the family hired another pet sitter, that person would echo my concerns, perhaps triggering some long-overdue improvements.

Being self-employed means a lot of things, not the least of which is protecting your reputation and constantly shaping the business to develop that reputation in a positive direction. One of the stickiest traps is falling in love with a pet that is in a bad situation, or whose human is difficult.

To the west, there's a charming old neighborhood along East River Road where a sweet, spoiled Yorkie lives. I was hired to walk him during his puppyhood, so he outgrew me. I still miss the rascal. I taught him to walk to heel, to sit, to stay – oh, my, what a wonderfully trainable boy. His human was a hoot, an attorney with more moxie than anyone has a right to. She would sometimes call me in the evening or weekend, with questions about his training. I'd say, "You just have to be smarter than he is." Her reaction at first was, "Excuse me, but you are speaking to someone who passed the bar." My response was, "Okay, that's one kind of intelligence. Another is in the display of his little round back when you give him a command. You *think* you're in charge. That little guy with the peanut-sized brain *knows* you're not."

When I work with puppies, I like to know what their humans are working on in the area of training, and what vocabulary they're using. This can be commands, but other things, too. Sometimes words such as "leash" or the name of a toy need to be reinforced. When I asked the Yorkie's human to leave me a short list of common words she was using with him, I had to wait for several days for a response. It was actually a note on her kitchen counter, saying, "I tried to write down the 'vocabulary' I use with Duffy. I felt so stupid, writing down things like 'moozy –woozy- fuzzy –wuzzy.' You know? It's a little embarrassing. And anyway, how do you spell that sort of thing?" I called her later to make my concerns clearer.

One more thing about Duffy and his human. People tend to assume that my business grows because clients tell others about me. That has almost never been the case. When I have asked clients to talk me up, I get some version of the following: "If I tell everyone about you, someday you'll be too busy for us. So we'll just keep you a secret." For quite a while, this was frustrating. Finally, I learned to respond, "If no one knows I'm here, someday I won't be available to you, because I'll be out of business." I thought that might get people to see my point of view, but it hasn't worked.

The Yorkie's human apparently never even told her very best friend about me. That person also happened to be a client of mine. These two women could have been sisters. They were matched for appearance (blond and petite)and temperament (high energy and argumentative). They were both attorneys. One day over lunch they got into an argument over who had the better pet sitter. They were apparently on the verge of getting their pet sitters together and putting them through some kind of test to prove the superiority of one or the other. I can only imagine their facial expressions when they found out I was pet sitter to both of them. "Word of mouth" does not work in my world, and that remains a challenge for me.

Right about now, I get tired of the bad music on the radio. I ward off ear worms by playing tunes from my inner jukebox. I think of songs or artists I like, then put them together mentally in some unlikely pairing. Since I am not a musician or even a sophisticated listener of music, this is quite an exercise for me. For example, I don't know whether Aretha Franklin has ever sung Billy Strayhorn's "A Flower Is a Lovesome Thing" but I do my best to bring it up in my head. It sounds quite good, by the way. The effort to put it all together completely obliterates commercial jingles and bubblegum music. Lately I've been trying to find good selections for Art Garfunkle and Johnny Cash. Of course, I want just the right song, something no one would have thought of. Otherwise, what's the point? The more unlikely the match-up, the better it is for drowning out the truly bad stuff.

We'll catch this entrance ramp and go straight into Oberlin. When this highway was being extended to the outskirts of town, there was the predictable mess where it came out on Rt. 20. On the south side of the road, the project involved tearing down some of the junky houses and a shabby night spot which I believe was called The Point. For quite a while, a deep slop-filled ditch ran along the front as well.

One Friday night I was going out for dinner with my then-spouse. I was vaguely aware that a little boy was standing at the edge of the ditch, seeming to toss a large rock repeatedly into the muck. Said my companion, "That boy has a cat." "No," said I, "it's a rock." Said he, "It's a cat. I think we should do something." I was ready to relax after an especially draining week (no week in social work is easy), and I knew that "we" actually referred to me. I had no strength for one more problem, or so I thought. My companion stopped the car and looked at me. Fine. I looked over, and that "rock" was looking right back at me, trying to blink the muck out of its eyes. His little legs were splayed, as if bracing for the next plunge. The boy had the kitten firmly by the skin of his back and, as I jumped from the car, slammed him into the slop once again.

"Hey!" I couldn't believe the kid would do this in front of witnesses. "What are you doing to that cat?"

"Just playin'." Fair enough. Stupid question, stupid answer.

"Well, give him to me."

"He's mine."

"He isn't yours to mistreat. Animals can be your best friends. Don't you know that?" I wanted to go on with my righteous indignation, but as I studied the boy's face and arms, I realized I was looking at an organic landscape of bruises and wounds in different stages of healing. I extended my arm. "Give me the cat. He deserves better."

The boy shrugged and put the dripping cat, a tiny kitten actually, into my hand. I put the kitten on the floor of the car beside my feet, and I got him back home without getting sewage all over my linen dress. And yes, I left that boy by the side of the road, feeling fairly certain that he needed rescuing, too. Unfortunately, such an accomplishment would be far more difficult. I made a mental note to contact a social work friend who worked in child welfare. With any luck, his family was known to the authorities or soon would be.

We were now late for dinner with another couple, and "kitten rescue" is one lame excuse to people who don't care about animals. I confined the kitten in a large carrier on the screened porch, and took off for the restaurant again. I had misgivings about saving the kitten. He didn't appear to have any physical injuries, which had been my first concern. Yet he probably was going to be nearly psychotic. Who could withstand that kind of treatment and not be affected forever? If we hadn't intervened, that little guy would surely be out of his misery by now. Instead, I told myself, I had just sentenced myself to many years of dealing with a warped cat.

Back home, in jeans and a tee shirt, I prepared to scrub a sewage-sodden kitten on the porch. When I opened the carrier door, I saw what he had been doing while I was away. He stepped out of the carrier, a fluffy, peach –colored sweetie, with guard hairs that glittered golden in the low western light of evening. He had polished off the cat food and yogurt I had hastily shoved into the carrier earlier. He rubbed against me, purring, clearly unafraid. He had cleaned himself completely, and was apparently not sick from all the glop he had ingested. One of the children I never gave birth to was a little boy named Samuel, so this little kitty boy would be Samuel Gold.

That night, I left my new kitten tucked away safely in the kitchen, with a warm bed, his own small pan, water and some moist food. I blocked off the room with a baby gate, hoping he would decide on the pan as the most appropriate place to eliminate.

The next morning I was eager to check on him, and walked into a kitten-free kitchen. Uh-oh. Well, that was my first reaction, but then I smiled. That little monkey had to have scaled the baby gate and set off on an adventure of his own. I was destined to love that tiny mischief-maker.

Not finding him on the main floor, I worried that he may have gone through the pet door and tumbled down the basement steps. Opening the basement door, here's what I saw – his goofy round-eyed face looking at me from midway up the steps. He was too small to tackle the open steps, and was carefully walking up the stringer board like an acrobat on a tightrope. Even at the beginning, Sammy did things his own way. My nickname for him has always been "Monkey Man," and he earns the name every day.

Sammy's behavior includes actions that probably defy certain laws of physics, or if not, at least he manages to make me sound like a crazy lady when I describe them. I hope I have a chance to point out one of his amazing feats before the day is over. That's all I'm going to say about that. He's just a magical cat. That's all. 'Nuf said.

CHAPTER 8

1:15 You Don't Want
a Dog Like This

Terrific – all times are approximate in the animal world, but at 1:15, we're right on schedule. We're going to see a Bichon Frise who lives in college housing. His human is an administrator of some sort, and an outstanding pet steward. This is a situation where a high-maintenance pet seems to be receiving everything he needs for maximum health and happiness.

I'm just sorry we couldn't bring Maggie. She adores Clinton – that's the Bichon – and they walk together when the conditions are right. When we walk across campus, their contrasting appearance brings them far more attention than they ever would receive individually. Besides, walking that sweet twelve-pound Bichon and my sixty-pound Lab is always good practice for me. I keep them both under control, with Maggie on a six-foot leather lead, and Clinton on a retractable lead that goes out at least twelve feet. Learning to coordinate that was actually a lot of fun.

Here we are. Now see that? Every pet sitter loves that sight. He's sitting on the back of the couch, his head poking through the lace curtain panels, watching for me. No need to go in quietly.

"Hey, Clinton! How's my little boy? Oh, gimme kiss. Oh, yes, I'm glad to see you, too. Ready to walk? What a silly question. Oh, yes, it is. Hold still, circus dog, while I get your lead clipped on. Sit. Good boy. Okay. Let's get out of here." And we're off, into this breezy September afternoon.

Clinton goes with me readily and happily, as long as his human isn't home. At times she is, and the experience is so different. She adopted him from a breeder who had received him back from his first adoptive family after a year. Clinton has the anxiety of any dog whose heart has been broken. When his human is home, he does not want to leave her, no matter how I try to reassure him or distract him as I coax him out the door. Early on, I asked her, "Should we put him through this?" Her answer was quick and certain. "Yes, I want him to learn that we may sometimes part, but we will always come back together."

Over time, Clinton has become less anxious, but he is not truly secure. Carol Lea Benjamin, in her marvelous training book *Second-Hand Dog* states, "The second-hand dog is second-hand for all his life." If only more people understood that. A widely held notion is that animals don't remember their experiences with us, but I don't think they forget anything. Benjamin's statement reinforces my belief. So we'll work on Clinton's separation anxiety, with a realistic goal of seeing it diminish.

Every coin has two sides, and while walking across campus is an intense socialization experience for Clinton, it is also his big chance to dive for abandoned food in the shrubbery. Like any animal, he sniffs out delectable morsels of garbage long before I see them. Big advantage for him. Clinton has found cheeseburgers, fried chicken, French fries, cookies, pie crust, and various unidentifiable substances. He understands "Drop it" and usually complies. Of course, he shoots me that same look that most dogs do. It says, "Why can't you find your own?" Then he looks puzzled when I throw his "find" into the nearest trash receptacle.

Clinton has allergies, some of them food-based, so I am watchful. Okay, here comes a middle-aged woman with that I-adore-your-dog look.

"What an adorable dog! She's a poodle mix, I guess?"

"Actually, he's a Bichon Frise. I think the breed has some relatives in common with the poodle."

"Where did you get him? I just have to have one."

"He isn't mine. I'm his dog walker. Here's my card. He's fairly high maintenance –"

"Oh, I can't believe that. He's so little and sweet."

"Yes, they're a companion breed, as opposed to a sporting or working breed, very appealing, but what dog isn't? He needs to be with you –or with someone- most of the time. Bichons don't do well languishing at home alone. Does your work take you away from home?"

"Oh, sure, I'm a musician. I travel a bit, but I work here at the college. So, if I had a dog, he would only have to be alone about eight or ten hours a day, like any other."

"That is normal, but that's my point. You can't leave a Bichon. I'm walking this little guy today because his human couldn't come home for lunch. She's attending an all-day training. Ordinarily she would be at home for lunch and give him a short walk. He doesn't do eight-hour stretches."

"Every day? That seems a little extreme."

"She does it faithfully. By the way, he gets filtered water, premium food, and a trip to the groomer every three or four weeks. Their fur is a lot like our hair. It grows endlessly, so you can't fudge on the grooming." Oh, here comes the shadow over the eyes.

"This all sounds like so much. I would just want an easy dog. You know, 'wash-and-wear.'" Now this is getting uncomfortable. Time to move on.

"Right. I don't blame you. Let me say this before we take off. You don't want a dog like this. Have a lovely day. C'mon, buddy."

Sweet, smart, funny, affectionate. And no dander, so he'll never make you sneeze. What's not to like? "Clinton, you're a lovin' sweetie, but some people would not be able to love you back in kind."

Nice woman, and she certainly would seem to have the resources to take care of a dog. The problem is, most people shouldn't have dogs. We – and I mean we- have a load of idealized notions about them. Growing up with dogs myself, I remember that they seemed to require no care or training. Okay, I'm pulling your leg a little. I grew up out in the township a long time ago, when it seemed there were no laws about animal control. Most dogs ran free, barked and howled at night, got into people's trash, killed Old Man Marshall's chickens, and were hooligans in general. We kids played tag with them, took naps on the sun-warmed lawn with them, and shared our ice cream with them. They loved us, guarded us, and looked fretful when we took parental scoldings for childish infractions. They were our perfect friends.

The dogs of my childhood seemed through my young eyes to be a lot like Lassie, that well behaved creature we watched on TV when the weather was too bad to play outside. Of course we had no idea of the extensive training such dogs were subject to, or how much grooming was required, and all the rest. We all know better now though, right?

Sometimes I think we have such a fascination with the animal world, we cannot be truly rational about it. We place animals in a false position. We treat them as lesser creatures, even though we know very little about them. What we don't understand about them, we want to believe doesn't matter or doesn't exist. It wouldn't hurt us to bring a little humility to our interest in animals. An open heart and an open mind are necessary for learning, and the animals are fine and willing teachers.

"Hey, Clinton. Hey, baby man, what are you chewing on? Give it. Give." No dice. Okay, and he's still chewing. I see a flash of green.

"C'mon, sweetie. Give it. Give it." It isn't a food wrapper. Oh, sure, bubble gum, a great big bright green wad. He's bound to drop it sooner or later.

Hah! He stops, walks backwards three steps with his head down, and then looks up at me, still chewing.

"What? You can't get rid of it, can you?" He's chewing slowly, ruminating almost. "It gives you such a thoughtful air." Stop. Three steps back slowly. He looks from side to side. "Give it. Oh, sure, clamp your jaws shut. I'm not competing for it. Honest." Two steps back, head down. Now a full stop.

"Clinton, that won't work. Just give it. Either that or I'm going to have to carry you. We'll never get home at this rate." He looks so puzzled. I'm sure he wonders why his efforts at mastication aren't breaking down this "food."

"You're not spending the afternoon blowing bubbles, young man. We're almost home, and I'll pry that out of your mouth if I have to."

Ordinarily Clinton would have shown off his great mastery of his retractable lead. I am not a fan of the things myself, since they are not suitable for most dogs or most situations. Obviously, the walker of a dog so tethered is not interested in the dog walking to heel, and has no other concerns about control or safety. Clipping a retractable lead to Clinton's collar for a romp across campus makes sense because he can be free to wander somewhat. We encounter almost no traffic and Clinton is not predatory, so I don't have to worry about pulling him back quickly.

A problem that often arises in the best of circumstances is that a dog will run the lead out as far as it will go, when he is unpleasantly lurched to a halt. Clinton doesn't have that experience. Just as the lead is about to run out, Clinton breaks from a trot to a stroll. He does this every time. When I've caught up with him, he may trot a bit more, but in any case he always knows where the end of that cord is. I can only guess that he is using judgement based on sound. This may seem like no big deal, but I've walked a lot of dogs on retractable leads, and he is the only one in my experience who has mastered the no-lurch technique.

"Okay, my sweet, we're home. Let's unhook this, so you can get some water. And you can't drink water until you give up the gum. Aren't you ready to give it? Aha! There it is. Thank you. Yes, you're a good boy." That is truly disgusting. And I'm changing that water right now. He is still the cutest thing.

"Hey, Clinton, I'm going now. Be good boy. I love you, little man."

CHAPTER 9

1:50 Della

If parking weren't a problem, we could sprint to the next dog walk. If my Oberlin business ever picks up, I'll get a bike and pedal to every stop. We're just going around the corner to Cedar Street.

Running a small business is so personal. When it's good, I'm just a little full of myself. When it hits a slump, I'm depressed. I once mentioned this emotional roller coaster to Gail the groomer. She sounded almost like my friend Frank. "Your business is your baby, your friend and your pay check. Every day people seek out or reject your services. If they become regulars, it's because they like you and trust you. Why wouldn't it feel personal?"

Yes, Gail was good to me – promoted me, you know. I left cards on her counter, and for a time she gave away little bags of homemade dog biscuits (yes, I made them) with my card attached. Several other groomers appreciated having a nice little give-away for their clients, too, and my cards got circulated.

Here we are. We're going to see Della, the maddeningly headstrong Golden retriever. Sometimes we walk, and sometimes we play in her fenced back yard. It's her decision.

"Oh, sweetheart! You are always right at the door. Oh, yes, you are. What a good girl. No. Leave the sleeve alone. Della, leave it." Goldens may be the most stubborn breed. Someday she will learn not to chew clothing, I hope. "Leave it. Good girl." That wasn't too bad, and this is after all the shirt she's already punctured.

"Where to? Out the back? Okay. Let's go." Looks like no walk today. Sometimes she likes to chase a toy, but she may just lie in the sun today. When we walk, she stops often, waiting for a treat. I am opposed to treat-based relationships, and here's where I practice my regal alpha look. She will stop and stare at my hands, waiting for a biscuit. I look off to the horizon, as if The Enemy might be coming up over the hill. After a while, Della tires of that and we walk some more. Her humans have allowed her to expect a treat every few feet, and I don't carry treats. Walking is its own reward.

"Oh, pretty girl, what is it, Della? You don't want to stay out? But it's such a pretty day." So we go in, and I'll try to get her to walk. Back door is yard, front door is walk.

"Want to walk? Get your leash." No dice. "Okay, the mail has come. Shall I read you a story?"

The humans apparently dress well, judging by the clothing catalogs. "Della, it's either this boutique-y thing or Talbot's. C'mon, let's cuddle up on the floor. Here we go." We'll "read" the same story I've been telling Lady forever.

"Once upon a time there was a beautiful young woman who lived in a house in the woods. When the night was warm and the moon was just right, she would leave the house and walk through the woods-what? Tummy rub? Sorry, I forgot."

"Anyway, the young woman was a changeling, and as she walked the moonlit path, she turned into a Golden retriever. As a woman, she needed beautiful skirts, blouses, sweaters, and shoes. As a retriever, she was perfectly attired in her splendid golden fur. What now? Chin scratch? I was just getting started here. Don't you like the story? This is all the farther we ever get anyway. Someday we'll talk about how the young woman tries to become a forever dog, because she's tired of changing back and forth. What is it, sweetheart? Oh, that's right. You never had your treats. You do get three of those, just for being you. Clever of you, too, since this is more than you would get on a walk."

Here's how I learned that Goldens can count to three. I never had permission to give Della three treats, but it seemed like a good number. The treats are those little bite-sized items, so what's three? That went on for some time. Well, I began to feel uneasy. After all, her humans are quite exacting in their expectations, and they had specified that two treats were the limit. I tried to reduce her intake back to two. Della would follow me to the front door, bumping my legs and my hands with her head as if to say, "Where's the rest?" I couldn't leave until I had given her three treats, and no other number. Yes, I tested that, too. A fourth treat caused a look of pity to wash over Della's face. Her poor pet sitter apparently couldn't count to three.

Della is the dog responsible for my wearing my raggedy denim shirt today, because she so often grabs clothing in her teeth and will not release. No clothing should be considered a proper chew toy. Della's humans began to learn this lesson one day when I was here. Ted dropped by the house to change clothes for a charity event. When he walked through the door and bent to hug Della, she got hold of his beautiful silk tie. I like pretty things, so I hoped the tie wouldn't be destroyed; nevertheless, Della was teaching Ted something I had not been able to do. I rather enjoyed listening to Ted, begging Della to let go. He and his wife had always found my complaints about Della's destruction of my clothing to be mildly amusing. Dogs don't have a way to distinguish between a silk tie and a ratty denim shirt. No amount of begging or scolding will change that. Chewing clothing has to be off-limits, period.

Here's something about the business that I would never have anticipated. I rarely see Della's humans, because they leave a check for me on the kitchen counter every week. I remember what they look like because their wedding picture is on display. I come and go five days a week, bringing in mail and packages, and spending about half an hour walking or playing with Della. I see Ted occasionally, walking Della around town in the evenings or on the weekends. Sometimes I wave, and I get a blank stare.

One Saturday I was checking out of the grocery store line, and Ted was in the next line. When he looked my way, I said "Hi, Ted." He returned my greeting with that frozen smile that says "I wish I could remember who you are." I understood.

As I walked across the parking lot, I saw that a woman in an SUV was trying to control her dog. When she saw me, she started laughing. The dog was trying to jump out the window. The woman said, "You must be Diana." Ted had reached the car, and looked first at Della, then at me. He laughed. 'Yes, you must be Diana. I've never seen Della behave this way."

One more thing, and I'll stop slobbering about Della. Ted once said, "If long life were the reward for goodness, dogs would live forever." Amen, brother.

"Della, our time is up. You don't seem to have touched your water, so I'll leave it. I love you, pretty girl. Yes, you could be Miss America. Pretty, pretty, pretty. Be good now."

CHAPTER 10

2:30 Errands and Chores

I need to run to the grocery store and then home. When I started the business, I had been broke for a while. After the business caught on- and it did so quite suddenly - I arrived home one night about nine o'clock. I completed my evening chores and took a bath. I was quite hungry, after walking about five or six miles that day, and working non-stop since early morning. I had developed a hearty appetite, and I was disappointed to see that the refrigerator was efficiently chilling a rotting green pepper and a stale heel of bread. The cupboard held coffee, tea, sugar and flour. What I would have given for a cold slice of pizza or some crunchy veggies. This dismal scene had been the norm for a long time, but now I was awash in money, with no way to get food! Such is life in a sleepy Midwestern town. Everything closes at 9:00. I quickly learned to organize myself quite differently, so the fridge and the cupboards now always have plenty of food.

A business is like a living thing, always growing or changing, or it is dying. I've said before that I take care of the business and the business takes care of me. I had run out of food because I was investing all my time and energy in the business. I guess everything has to be balanced, too. If I ever get so busy that I can't comfortably find time to shop, I'll do what I learned years ago in a corporate training workshop. The speaker said, "Don't waste precious time doing what you can pay someone else to do." At some point, I'll need housekeeping, lawn care, a shopper, and – hey!- someone to bake pie.

Oh, good. A spot not too far from the entrance. I walk enough in a day! And I can't stand long lines.

I have a beautiful eggplant at home, and everything for eggplant parmesan except bread crumbs. Now here's what mystifies me about finding bread crumbs in the store. I suspect grocery stores are organized by people who have never cooked, and perhaps have never even stumbled into a kitchen. It's too much to ask for bread crumbs to be in the bread aisle, but maybe they could be near something that bread crumbs are used on. Store planners always have several shadowy areas where they assign space to items that make them say, "Ooh, goody, more miscellaneous." Only cashiers with ten-year pins can tell you where to find them.

Let's see – I think I remember finding bread crumbs in the canned vegetable aisle. First, I dip down the pet food aisle, just to see what they're selling. Most of the "food" has too much grain, dyes and chemicals. You wouldn't live on stuff of this quality, so don't expect your pets to do so. You could wait until they complain. Oh, that's right – they don't complain – ever. That's one of the reasons we like them. Let's not exploit that trait. Feeding your pets the best food you can afford means you'll have fewer vet bills for sickness-related visits. Your pet will live longer and will feel better. I have seen behavior problems in multiple-cat households virtually disappear with an upgrade in the pet food. I'm always ready to be pleasantly surprised at the addition of a wholesome product, but that hasn't happened today. Same old line-up.

I like looking at the pet toys, too, so I can still say to my clients with certainty that they shouldn't be buying that stuff. Flimsy dog toys that end up in puppy tummies, and cat toys that in no way resemble prey. Hard plastic balls, jingle bells, and those ugly little mice with glued –on features should simply not be made. They will continue to be made because people still buy them. We should all be avoiding these grocery store pet aisles, unless, of course, we're spying.

Yep, here are my bread crumbs, hovering over the canned veggies. I'm having a vegetable entrée tonight, although I'm not a vegetarian. I have been at times, but everything can be politicized. When I was a young adult, I became a vegetarian and therefore a two-headed weirdo as far as my family was concerned. I decided that if I was going to make holiday dinners at my mother's less uncomfortable, I would go back to eating meat. I thought that it was better to be able to eat whatever was served to me wherever I was. At that point in my life, I anticipated a decades-long semi-public life with friends and colleagues, gathering together at dinner parties, fundraisers, and heaven knows what events. Picking at my food would not be prudent.

Now that I make my living taking care of animals, some people think I should not eat meat. The unavoidable truth is I'm an omnivore. I eat very little meat, maybe a meat entrée twice a month. A friend of mine always buys great hunks of beef on those Styrofoam trays, and she makes sure there's no sign of bone or fat. That way she can pretend that those squishy red squares are something other than the flesh of an animal. Here's how I straightened out my attitude about eating meat. Before I begin eating, I thank the animal for giving his life so I can be nourished. That animal is likely a chicken or a turkey, since I do restrict my intake to feather food. That single step of being mindful that I'm about to consume something that once could have looked me in the eye makes me appreciative. I recommend it to anyone who still eats meat. You may find that you'll eat only when you're hungry and not overdo it. If only that worked for pie.

As long as I'm here, I'll pick up these salt-free rice cakes. Maggie loves a bite-sized piece of rice cake smeared with peanut butter as her nighttime snack. Let's get through this check-out before a line forms.

While I'm transacting this, let me just say, this is a good life. I wouldn't recommend pet sitting as a living. It simply isn't for everyone. You must truly like animals and they must like you. You have to be fit enough to handle the physical demands of working with animals. Just hanging out with pets is wonderful fun, but you have to have the strength, skill and knowledge to manage creatures who are often faster, stronger and smarter than you. Some of that skill comes from experience and some comes from ongoing education about the nature of the animals you care for.

I've brought you along on a relatively uncomplicated day, but quite often there are other chores involved. I routinely bring in mail and packages, water houseplants, and in summer water whole vegetable gardens. More than ever people are running dehumidifiers year-round, and I empty those, too, when necessary. One Christmas day, when snow and heavy winds caused serious drifting, I shoveled eighteen driveways just to get to the pets in my care (yes, some of them were the same driveways over again!).

A glass of wine at dinner is out, too, because there is the occasional call regarding medical emergencies. Clients have called to say they are on the way to the hospital, and instruct me to "take Maxie out tonight , tomorrow morning, and until I tell you to stop." Sometimes the client calls to ask if I can rush their pet to the emergency veterinary services clinic. Of course, I drop whatever else I'm doing. I keep my eye on the weather, not just because I'll be out in it, but because heavy rains and wind may cause damage to the homes of clients who are out of town. I have had to call for help with flooded basements and fallen tree limbs. I do, however, shut off my phone after 9:00pm. A girl needs her rest.

A pet sitter is more than happy to work every day of the year, contributing to the happiness and well-being of pets. A pet sitter appreciates the people who care about their own pets. If you are a good pet sitter, you are the best person you know to be trusted with people's precious pets and access to their homes.

A couple of reasons not to start a pet sitting business would be wanting to avoid people and looking for ready cash. People have to like and trust you. This is a fact lost on people who have never used the service. Complete strangers have actually said to me, "I'd love to do what you do. I hate people." That used to leave me dumbstruck, but now I say, "That will work well for you when animals write the checks."

As for ready cash, even in a healthy economy a business based on trust is built slowly. There's that trust factor again- it all goes back to the people. The animals must rely on us, the people, to do well by them. A pet sitter must be a partner every day in that collaboration of loving care.

Let's get across town now. This is my chance to catch up on personal chores and check up on my own sweethearts. Long-time clients know this is a sort of lull for me, so calls often come in between 3:00 and 4:00. I'm somewhat expecting a woman to call, one who came home three days early. She knows that I don't give refunds, but she thought I would make an exception in her case. She came home because she found her vacation destination a huge bore. I sympathize, but she paid for my availability. My policies and practices are shaped in part by experiences with clients. When the business first took off, I was fairly casual in my dealing with clients. At that time, I was paid after the work was completed. A family came home early, on a Friday afternoon. I couldn't fill the weekend slots at that point, but I could have if I had known. So, instead of having paying customers and customers I had to turn away, I now had clients who returned early with no obligation to pay, and clients I lost because they had made other arrangements. I lost twice. I am now paid in advance. If people return early because of circumstances beyond their control, I will carry a credit for them. The advance payment also throws cold water on those deadbeats who never planned to pay me in the first place. If you're wondering, I had just one such experience.

Sometimes the situations aren't as clear-cut or as obvious. For a time, I had a few clients who called for pet care the day before holiday weekends began. These were all long-time clients. I always say that I work every day, but there have been times when my holiday schedule was light and I accepted invitations to various events. The last-minute demand for pet sitting services made me feel happy for the business and disappointed for myself that I had to cancel my own plans. After a time, one of those clients admitted that she hired me under those circumstances only when her maid reneged at the last minute on an agreement to care for the pets. I learned that that was the case across the board. Okay. Time to institute a holiday fee for late reservations. If they wanted my services at the last minute, they would pay time and a half. From my side of the equation, if my personal holiday plans were going to be cancelled, at least I had extra money in my pocket.

I once used a tactic used by many businesses, but I did not carry it off successfully. When I did not want someone's business, I quoted the prospective client a higher rate than I thought she would be willing to pay. Well, that one was a pie in my own face. The rate wasn't high enough, and the woman agreed to it. I ended up working in a difficult situation (although I adored the dog). Lesson learned.

Okay, we're home. Now I get to see my own sweethearts.

"Hey, Maggie! Wagga-wagga, oh, yes. You are a love. Did we get any calls? You'll never tell." A quick check of voice mail tells me we have three calls. Let me play these through while I change the pets' water.

"Hello. My vet gave me your number. We've been thinking of leaving our dog at home when we go away for a few days...."

"Yes, I'm the concierge at a new condo complex, and your message mentions Lorain County. Do you come into Cuyahoga? I have new residents inquiring about dog walking...."

"Hi. We have a brand new puppy and we're going to a four-day conference. My husband thinks he's too young to stay at a kennel..."

Well, thank God the husband is making sense. Let's call them before they do something rash. Let me get their number. Here we go. "Hi. This is Diana Carter, the pet sitter. You called about puppy care? .....Eight weeks old? .....Yes, they're a handful....Your first dog? Oh, my.... Yes, they will take everything out of you for a while. How long have you had him?....Four days. Did you know when you brought him home from the breeder's that you were going out of town?....I see. So this is a continuing education event, and the same thing is offered every three months... Why did you and your husband both decide to go at the same time? ...Ha! Yes, I know what a bore it can be. Here's the problem. You have a baby in the house....You had that intuition about it? Good. Trust your intuition. I don't like to turn down business, but I feel strongly that that puppy needs to bond with you right now.... Yes, I would strongly suggest it. If you can do this conference when it's offered again, or if just one of you goes this time, the puppy will be better off. Ideally, you should both be with him....Yes, if the two of you are his new "pack," you should both be there to show him that. He needs to feel secure, and so far he's had a little over eight weeks to figure out the world....then he also has to get to know you....I'm sure you'll do the right thing....Yes, thanks for calling. Keep my number. I look forward to meeting you at some point, and taking care of your dog when he's ready. Bye now."

Disaster averted, I hope, unless a well-meaning friend insists on taking care of him. I think she understood, though. She sounded very caring. That isn't the first time I've been called when a difficult situation arose involving puppy care. Adopting a puppy is a bit like giving birth to a baby. There is never a convenient time to do it. If you want the experience (and there are no rational reasons to do so), you just have to dash into it with your arms and your heart wide open. After the initial warm hug, reality sets in and the work begins.

All right, the other calls can wait. Let's run the vacuum upstairs. I'm going to "hit the high spots" as my mother used to say. With my pet sitting schedule, there's no such thing as a large block of time for cleaning. For serious cleaning, I created a system. I go through the house, a room at a time, giving myself a whole month for each room. That sounds like a lot, but I take each room completely apart, not just cleaning but doing any necessary maintenance as well. I have to break up the tasks so that I can work in short time periods. The system works well for me, since I love a clean house but hate to clean it.

Ah, we have two kitties on the bed. Katherine and Shadow are taking their afternoon nap curled up together, and we'll have to disturb it. "Oh, my dears, you'll want to leave." Sleepy looks, but they know the signal. "Whooshka! Whooshka!" And away they go. We flip on the sweeper, and all kitties are out of the room. Who says cats can't be trained? Before I developed that warning for my cats, their startled reactions caused some unfortunate results, piddling and broken lamps being the worst. I'm a fanatic about vacuuming and owning the best vacuum I can afford. I learned a long time ago that vacuuming faithfully and washing pet bedding weekly are the best ways to prevent a flea infestation. Once you've got 'em, you have to bring in chemicals. Prevention is so much better for so many reasons.

In my work, I can't afford to be the Typhoid Mary of Fleas. Imagine how my business would go down if I were taking fleas into clients' homes. Now that rug looks so much better. I'll hit the spare room tomorrow when I have more time.

And here we have Maggie and Herbie cuddling on the couch. Herbie is Maggie's cat. I suppose I would have adopted Herbie eventually, but Maggie took a special interest in him.

Every year in the spring and early summer, the shrubbery of Oberlin howls, whimpers and meows. It isn't hoodoo. We're just hearing from desperate pets, apparently abandoned by college students. That's the prevailing theory anyway, since these strays are a cut above. Most of them have been spayed or neutered, and tend to be well socialized and well mannered.

A couple of years ago I saw Herbie about two doors away at a student rental, crying to get in at the back door. He knew where home was, but the place was vacant as of the end of May, and nobody would live there again until the following August. The landlord chased Herbie off the porch one day with a broom, but Herbie went right back. He knew where he belonged. I felt sorry for him, but I had plenty of cats.

Herbie was not just determined; he was resourceful. One day when I was hanging clothes on the line, our hedge of lilac bushes began to cry. The sound was rather bird-like, and I wondered whether someone had lost or abandoned a caged bird. Maggie investigated. She bravely stuck her nose into the hedge. The crying stopped. Maggie stepped back. The crying began again. Maggie moved toward the hedge, and the crying stopped again. Herbie's white face poked out of the hedge for a moment. Maggie looked back at me. I had finished my chore and was watching Maggie and the cat with fascination. I was well aware of my dog's gentle nature and her intelligence. She was taking on something, all on her own. She was going to handle it better than I would have. I have already admitted to you that I knew about Herbie but had not tried to help him.

Maggie lay down, sphinx-style. She was facing away from me, and I could only go by her body language to sense her level of focus. Her ears, although in a normal position, seemed to quiver. She was otherwise motionless. Herbie's face showed, and then receded. He continued to appear and disappear in this manner for about twenty minutes, until he realized that Maggie was now sitting still. Herbie began to come out, revealing a beautiful classic tabby coat and four white feet. Finally, Maggie rolled over on her side. Maggie had learned as a growing puppy that lying on her side was the least threatening position for the cats. They would curl up against her tummy and sleep. She was now using this position to make a new friend.

Eventually, Herbie moved into the house, and he is now showing signs of being one of the Great Ones. All cats are fascinating, but some cats are more special than others. And Herbie still makes that piercing caged bird sound, especially when I'm on the phone. I suppose he thinks that it makes no sense for me to be standing in the kitchen talking into a piece of plastic. I should be preparing food, at the very least, or using my free hand to pet him.

You might think he's just a classic tabby with Bette Davis eyes and an overworked sense of entitlement, but no one tops him for intelligence and speed. He has standards, too, expecting to be the first to use a freshly cleaned pan. He has a passion for white cheddar cheese and fresh catnip. I can pick up Herbie and cuddle with him, not something every cat welcomes. He tucks his head under my chin and gives out a smooth, steady purr. He plays full-out rough with Cujo, and plays only gentle tapping games with the ladylike Katherine Katz. Sweet, smart, and classy. I'm glad Maggie chose him.

CHAPTER 11

4:10 Folly's Afternoon Walk

Enough of that. Let me get some coffee together and we'll head out again. It's that time of day when my energy level may sag a bit, so I put cold coffee in a cup with milk and chocolate syrup. Somehow that combination really wires me.

Now that I think of it, when Maggie was a boisterous puppy she and Katherine Katz became friends through a kind of hide-and-seek game like the one Herbie used with Maggie. The difference was that Maggie was the newcomer, and out of control at that. Katherine got tired of running through the cat door to get away from Maggie. One day after a romp through the house, she turned and stuck her head through the "door." This was actually a little gingham curtain that covered a kicked-out panel in the old wooden basement door. Maggie could stick only her head through the opening, and often did so in a futile attempt to follow.

When Maggie pulled her head out of the cat door, Katherine at first stuck only her head out, and then after a while began to stand halfway out of the door. Over the course of a few days, Maggie learned that she had to control herself if she wanted Katherine to come out to stay. This was a fundamental lesson for any dog, and it demonstrated Maggie's intelligence. She had to rein in her canine (overwhelming) nature, and copy Katherine's feline (restrained) nature. When Katherine would show herself, Maggie would lie down on her side and wait for the kitty to come to her. Katherine's determination to create a friendship with a slobbering, galumphing beast was a great gift to Maggie, who eventually learned to make friends with all kinds of creatures by mirroring their ways. Clearly Katherine was quite savvy, too, for she saw Maggie's sweetness behind the wild antics.

Let me grab my cold coffee and we're out. "Bye, Maggie. We'll go again when it's cooler. Take care of the kitties. I love you so, good girl." I don't know why I say anything, except that it makes me feel better. She already knows she can't go with me, and my string of words doesn't mean anything to her. If ever I am guilty of anthropomorphizing my pets, it's at times like these.

We're on our way to see Folly again. He is a perfectly spoiled senior pet. Folly's human lets him out first thing in the morning and the last thing at night. I give him two half-hour walks every day, after breakfast and before supper, and that alone makes his exercise regimen better than that of many people I know. His diet isn't bad, either, and he never eats treats. I swear there are dog breeds prone to self-restraint, and the standard poodle is one. Folly is slim, strong, healthy, and beautiful.

Let's get onto the street and over to Kendal without hitting any straggling high school students. You know, my own Maggie has the same attributes I just listed for Folly. A major difference is in their attitude toward food. Actually, I've gradually changed the way I do everything in order to control Maggie's scavenging. Folly's human can throw food scraps in the wastebasket, and she can even walk away from her meal, trusting Folly not to touch it. I never turn my back on my food, and whatever I don't compost goes into the freezer until trash day. It's the only way to foil both Maggie's hunting through the wastebasket and the wildlife tipping over the trash can.

Before we get there, I have time to tell the story of Maggie and the cinnamon rolls. I understand what people mean when they say that animals don't lie, but can we also agree that they are capable of misrepresenting certain situations or their role in them? This is a story about my master food stealer.

My lightest schedule usually falls on a Sunday. People like to return from trips on Saturday or early Sunday to get ready for the week (yes, even the retirees, perhaps just a habit of mind). In cold weather, Sunday afternoon is my chance to make up batches of soups and chili and to bake scones and tea breads for the freezer. Then there's the pie of the week. Hey, who wants to put up with store-bought pie? It is a staple around here, and life is not worth living without all manner of homemade bakery. Well, one Sunday morning, I got tired of the talking heads on the tube, and decided to throw some cinnamon rolls together. No, not the old-fashioned kind where you have to get up at 4:00am, work with yeast, and spend three hours creating a little bit of heaven. And yes, I grew up eating those, but I don't have the skills or the patience necessary. I buy those frozen ones that just have to thaw a little before they go into the oven. On the morning in question, my sweet tooth was screaming and I was going to make a serious dent in a pan of goodies. Oh, yum, junk food fresh from my own oven.

While the rolls cooled on the counter top, I went upstairs to strip the bed and sort laundry. Because I have cats, I've learned to ignore random clunking sounds, such as the one I heard about five minutes into my chores. I finished my work and went downstairs, looking forward to rewarding myself with coffee and a warm cinnamon roll.

I passed through the living room, where Maggie was just as I had left her, sprawled out on the couch. She gave out a small yawn, clearly bored with the Sunday morning talking heads. That's my girl, I thought proudly. When we bring them up from puppyhood, they grow up to be so much like us.

Yes, in retrospect, I had distinctly heard that thud. And yes, that little yawn seemed a bit forced. I am as capable as the next person of clinging to an idea in spite of mounting evidence that it is hooey, and so I stopped in my tracks when I saw the baking pan in the middle of the kitchen floor. As I picked it up, I saw that - except for the fact that it had been sitting on the floor – the pan could have been put away. I ran my hand around the inside and across the bottom. My lovely non-stick pan bore not so much as a speck of cinnamon. Perhaps I had lost my mind. Perhaps I had not baked anything after all. Hah!

Cinnamon is good for us, humans and dogs alike. It is a natural "internal cleanser," I've been told. Well, my thoroughly cleansed mischief maker managed to recover from her overindulgence within a few days. Her lower GI distress was her punishment.

Had I caught her in the act, I would foolishly have said, "What are you eating?" I have in fact asked this stupid question so often, I plan to use it as the subtitle for Maggie's biography. Of course, asking in the first place is a violation of Carter's Law: "If you don't think you can handle the answer, don't ask the question."

Okay, let's drive carefully into Kendal. Sometimes cars nearly fly out of the employee parking lot.

Comparing Folly to Maggie, he is not a full-time scavenger, but he is also not passive or helpless. When he first moved here, his diet was rather poor. Twice he got away from his human, and both times, thanks to a configuration of sliding doors with motion sensors and swinging kitchen doors, he ran all the way through the main building and into the big kitchen. The cooks were astounded to see a pony-sized dog counter surfing. Once his diet was improved, he stopped his marauding. That's something we should all think about.

"Hey, Folly! You were right at the door, sweet boy. There's nothing like the classic doggie greeting to make a person feel welcome. Oh, yes, and you are better at it than many. That pom-pom tail does get a workout. Are you ready to walk? Let's clip on your leash and get out of here. Wait.

Let's take the back section of the newspaper. When we get to where we're going, I'll read the funnies to you."

We'll head out toward the east. Folly and I have a favorite spot for communing, and it's quiet and shady this time of day.

"You know, Folly, your friendship and the love of the other animals I see and their humans are everything to me. I don't know what my life would be now if I hadn't dreamed up this job. You think I'm just some woman who walks you twice a day, and of course you're right. But you, to me, represent a life-saving and life-changing development. I tell you this because I can't say these foolish things to anyone else. You don't laugh and you don't judge. Or if you do, you keep it to yourself. Some people say that they wish their pets could talk. Ha! Clearly they haven't thought it through."

Yes, I have told Folly everything. I'm sure people around here see me talking to Folly and wonder what the heck I'm saying. Maybe they think I'm putting him through some kind of intensive training. Well, no. Folly's my therapist. He knows all about my insecurities, my dreams, my major mistakes in life, and all that led me to where I am now. He could be my biographer. No one has heard more than he.

"Stay. Let's look out for those cars, my sweet. Okay."

We could walk in the grass, but we'll cross the road so we can walk on the sidewalk. Folly has enough arthritis that he prefers to walk on smooth surfaces now. I'm always impressed with how quickly dogs figure out what's best for them.

Let's keep our eyes peeled for flattened amphibians. Folly loves to scoop them up and crunch on them. I'm torn about it. They probably make a good snack for a dog, but knowing that doesn't make the vision less disgusting or distressing. This whole area was wetlands not long ago and the stunned wildlife sometimes wander around on the blacktop looking for an environment that makes sense to them.

"Ack!" There goes one now. "It's okay, Folly. It's okay. Don't mind me. Munch away. At least that little toad didn't die in vain." How did I miss that?

Notice how classy he is? No attempt whatsoever to roll in it first.

Once toads are flattened, either by car tires or those industrial-sized lawn mowers, they seem to become utterly desiccated very quickly. After all, we walk these grounds twice a day, and that toad was not there yesterday (we walked a different way this morning). Today he's a cracker. The blacktop is, of course, quite hot on sunny days.

I'm reminded that the hot blacktop is exactly why and when Folly started wearing boots, and not in winter but in the middle of summer. Kendal has great expanses of lawn, but plenty of blacktop, too. I discovered that sometimes I just couldn't get Folly from point A to point B without walking on the searing blacktop. Like most animals, he never complained, but he would sometimes hesitate and give me a mournful look before dashing across a parking lot. I bought him boots, and that took care of his problem as far as

I was concerned. The boots seemed expensive, but Folly's comfort is something I'm responsible for; besides, the boots were worth the price in hilarity to see Folly learning to walk in them. You may have seen it yourself when a dog first wears boots– that first cautious step, then a ten-second freeze while he hopes that odd feeling will go away, another step, then a short sprint intended to outrun that thing that has hold of all four feet. Sometimes there's a phase involving a splayed stance, accompanied by an expression of deep thought. After that, it's a slow recognition that whatever is wrong is semi-permanent and simply must be endured. Folly has never become completely comfortable in boots, so he wears them only in extreme heat or cold. I would prefer that nothing interfere with that dignified poodle gait.

I suppose some people think clothing for dogs is ridiculous. I would agree that some of it is, but when it comes to protection from the elements, I am all for boots and coats. My Lab wears a coat in winter when the temperature drops below 20 degrees. Yes, that may be an arbitrary standard, but I base it on how my dog behaves in the cold. I will admit I took a scolding from my vet when Maggie had some kind of doggie flu, and vowed to take better care of her in extreme weather. As the vet reminded me, our pets become acclimated to central heating just as we do. It seems obvious to me now, but I had a lot to learn then, and I'm learning still.

"Folly, if you had been someone's pet when I was a kid, you probably would be running loose right now. Sounds good, doesn't it? On the other hand, you might also know about the business end of a broom and what a kick in the ribs felt like. Pets usually lived outside and medical attention for them was almost unheard of. Imagine that. And they were always getting into mischief, harmless and otherwise."

In my childhood, township areas were undeveloped, with lots of woods and meadows, along with farmers' fields. Our pets had the freedom to run their legs off, interact with their own kind, and to hunt. We provided our pets with minimal shelter. Our own dog had a little house beside the garage and the cat was allowed into the laundry room on winter nights. Pets lived fully but briefly, dying from poisoning, gunshot wounds, or undiagnosed medical conditions. Some were hit by cars or died slowly and dreadfully out in the woods after being snared in a leg trap. They were not likely to be neutered or vaccinated; in short, they were subject to the best and the worst that Mother Nature handed out. Our elders, in the 1950's and 60's, still remembering an agrarian life, related to animals as creatures that more or less fended for themselves in fields or outbuildings.

For us children, our pets were our protectors, our nannies, our teachers, our confessors, and our playmates. We kids adored them. They deserved to be treated, at the very least, like the lesser gods of Olympus. And don't tell me I'm overstating anything. I would just have to say it again. I can only hope that somehow those divine creatures knew how important they were to us.

Today the problems are different for our protected indoor pets. Our challenge is to provide them with all the things they can't go out and get for themselves. We must see that they get enough exercise, and in the case of dogs, social interaction with people and other dogs. Because they can't hunt, and this is crucial for cats, we must give them the best food we can afford. We are all they have. I don't mean that in an arrogant way. On the contrary, that awareness can lead to real humility as we let them teach us how to care for them.

As we walk past this pond on our left, I always look for the heron. She must have a nest on that islet. Knowing next to nothing about feathered creatures, I don't even know when the best sighting times are. Seeing her take flight with that extraordinary wing span is always a breathtaking delight. No such luck today. We'll walk a little farther now and cross the road again to reach our destination. Tomorrow we'll come this way, stay on this side of the road, and take the looping path through the woods.

"Stay. Let's wait for that car." I give the Miss America wave, whether I know the driver or not. "Okay."

"Here we are, Folly. This is our very favorite shady spot and it's dry enough to sit down and enjoy it for a while. Sit down here, buddy, and let's get comfortable. " The sun is on the far side now, and a month or so ago, we treasured what a cooling place this can be to relax in the afternoon. The trees here are not part of a human landscaping scheme, but Mother Nature's own, mercifully left by the developers. The shorter stuff on the edges are the usual shrubs, red osier dogwood and common buckthorn. The big trees, some as high as sixty feet tall, are cottonwoods and oaks. Even though we're in September, the oaks have a long way to go before dropping leaves. The red oaks are prevalent here, and very common in Ohio, but I see something else. The great botany professor George Jones would be ashamed of me that I can't identify it, but I have forgotten much of what he taught me. Here's a leaf on the ground from one of those trees. It has the shape of an oak, but without the bristle tips. It's wavy, almost smooth, along the edges. Hmmm. There's something called swamp oak, or maybe swamp white oak. I'll look it up later. Dr. Jones always said that he couldn't remember people's names very well, but never forgot the name of a plant once he learned it. I'm the same way with animals.

"How about a tummy rub, Folly man? It's so peaceful here, sweet doggie. Hey, I brought the funnies to read to you. Let's see if there's a funny animal cartoon. Hmm, no. I don't see a thing today. Something must be happening to me –most of these comics I don't even understand."

"Oh, now this might be worth our while, Folly. Do you follow your horoscope? What? Was that an eye roll? Try to be open-minded. I forget when your birthday is. Sometime in the spring, no? Gemini? We'll have a look. 'Beware of an unexpected financial request on the part of a colleague or sibling. Make the choice that is right for you.' Well, that flies in the face of my suspicion that horoscopes usually fit dogs better than they do people. It goes on. 'Ongoing health issues come from emotional stress, not your diet.' You don't have stress anymore, Folly, and your diet, as we know, is becoming more organic every day. Maybe I have the wrong sign. When is your birthday? It's the twelfth of what? I know it – July. That's Cancer. Hmm. Let me think. Of course! That sign is you all over. Intuitive, loving, sympathetic, and at times overemotional. That is so you, my sweet. We'll test it. Here's Cancer for today. I hope it doesn't say not to eat toads.

"'Be willing to make adjustments to your schedule, even if it means extra effort on your part.' I don't see the relevance, do you? 'You may strengthen a relationship with a loved one when you eliminate your problems away from home.' Okay, that makes sense. Your human did say she wished you would poop on your walks and not near her patio."

"'Use your loving nature to head off a complaint coming your way.' Is there something I should know about? She did say something to me yesterday about how you stick your wet nose on her in the morning to wake her up. You could try to be more subtle."

"'Reward yourself tonight with your favorite snack food.' It would appear you've already done that. Folly, I think we have it. Cancer is definitely you. I think we're on to something."

"Okay, let's make our way back, old man. Can you get up? Good boy. Shake it off."

"Hey, what are you so excited about? Oh, it's one of your admirers. Folly, your tail is going to wear out. Hello, Nan!" He spotted her before I did, and he has cataracts. Must be his doggie nose at work.

Nan is one of the finest people I know and pretty as a movie star, and she and Folly just love each other. I swear he senses when she's within a quarter of a mile.

As she throws her arms around his neck, she says, "May I hug him? You know, my husband and I plan to get a dog just as soon as we stop traveling. " She always says this, and I always smile stupidly instead of responding, "But you know where to find a great pet sitter, so why wait?"

Folly is so excited, he's almost gasping. "Easy, buddy, this is your friend Nan. Don't get all worked up. Nan, you may hug Folly as much as you want. He loves you. In fact, he doesn't get this wound up over most people."

"Surely you're just saying that. But I do love dogs, always have. Oh, Folly, I just enjoy the feeling of that curly fur. All right, one more hug, then I'm off."

"Thanks, Nan. Folly is grateful for the attention."

"Oho! I'm grateful to have Folly around. See you soon." Nan's beautiful smile is for him, and she gives him one last loving pat before she takes off.

"There she goes, one of your biggest fans. Aren't you a lucky boy? Such wonderful attention just for being yourself." I'm just a little envious.

Folly's good will ambassadorship is effortless. He cheers everyone he meets, and they seem to do the same for him. As for dogs, they are hard-wired to be group animals. Surely the greatest form of poverty for a dog is the absence of meaningful interaction with people and others of his own kind.

Something about animals can bring out the best in us, and I don't mean that in a sentimental way. I don't know what I mean exactly, and maybe that's the larger point. There's something about animals that we don't understand. We feel it and are drawn to it, sometimes strongly, but we are dumb and blind in the presence of it. What is it? I can't begin to name it. The writer Henry Beston, in *The Outermost House*, writes about our relationship to the animal world. The partial quote I carry in my head from that book is, "[other species] are not brethren, they are not underlings; they are other nations caught with ourselves in the net of life and time." No wonder vets, groomers, pet care providers, trainers, and anyone who lives with animals are always learning.

Some of my clients have expressed a sense of inadequacy as stewards of their pets. I cringe inside when someone says, for example, "You probably think I'm a bad kitty mom." I have said to clients and I'll say it again, as long as we continue to learn and to give our pets the best we know how, we're okay. We can really beat ourselves up over practices we may have engaged in in the past. Shoot. Nobody looks good in that light. So much has changed. Pet food is better, as is vet care, grooming practices, and resources for education about pet care. Let's just keep getting better.

"Folly, let's get across the road here. Stay. Let's wait for the truck. Well, now, there goes someone in need of education. Aren't you lucky not to be that guy's dog? He's got a retriever mix – I'm guessing – in the back of his pick-up. I would never do that to you, Folly. And someday there will surely be a law prohibiting people from letting their dogs ride in the backs of trucks." Time to start teaching physics in schools. But what are the chances? That man must have no idea what would happen to the dog if the truck had to stop suddenly.

"Okay. Such a good dog, you are."

Or letting dogs stick their heads out of car windows. What are those people thinking? I, too, believe that animals are darn nearly magical, but I don't think some unearthly force protects them from all the things I need a windshield for.

"Folly, here we are at your door. I'll see you tomorrow. Remember, no matter what happens, I love you."

CHAPTER 12

4:45 Miss Kitty

We'll cut across this expanse of lawn and go over to Miss Kitty's place. I find myself loving these animals as much as I love my own. They're individuals, and they don't seem to be guileful enough to hide their quirks as well as people sometimes can. They save their guile for looking innocent when the Sunday roast or the birthday cake has some early samples taken out of it.

"Hey, Miss Kitty. I love that you greet me at the door. Did you hear me coming? Of course you did." I am constantly being reminded that my own hearing and sense of smell are just about worthless.

"What have you been up to, my sweet chubby love? Your fur is so smooth. Yes, you like to be petted. Tummy rub? Certainly." First things first. When Miss Kitty throws herself down in front of my feet, there is no ignoring her. "Feel good? My, that is one vast tummy. I'm hearing the faintest purr, but I also know I have to watch that tail. At the sign of the slightest flicker, this is over, my sweet."

Let me just do a quick check of everything. "Hey, girlie-girl, did you spit up anything?" Kitchen and living room look good…hallway is okay … bedroom looks good, too. I may as well change the pan while I'm here. Miss Kitty is an only cat, but she's at an age when she's urinating more heavily. Besides, a cat just likes a clean pan.

One of the things I love to rant about is dirty kitty pans. We bring cats into our homes, and sometimes only think we know what they need from us. The cat is a hunter in nature, and relies on lack of detection in order to capture his prey. That involves, among other things, being nearly odor-free, so our feline companions have very high standards of cleanliness. When you walk into a home and can smell cat pee, don't blame the cat. The least we can do is keep the pans clean. When we consider all that the cat has given up for the security of a life indoors, mucking out his pan for him every day is not a big deal. 'Nuf said.

Okay, I'm not ready to push my soapbox aside. I don't like those automated cat pans, and I have seen cats become litter pan-averse because of them. Of course, there are some cats that do well with them. They're more complicated and usually harder to clean than a plain pan that can be sanitized in minutes, so I'll retain my bias.

Let me say this about training cats to use a commode. A clever trick, no? It's impressive. And a few people have been successful in that training, but not many. Here's what I think. If you haven't taught your cat to do this, please don't think less of yourself. Digging up a storm in a cat box and covering up his own waste is one of the few satisfying and authentic activities the indoor cat still has. Let him enjoy it.

"What's this? What did you do? Miss Kitty, I told that cricket this morning that he was in a safe place. And whose body parts are all over the closet? That poor thing. Well, old girl, you've still got the killer instinct. Congratulations." Wow! Talk about satisfying and authentic. Hunting opportunities are truly rare.

"Why the funny stare? Yes, I found it. See? It's in my hand. Good girl. Big hunter. I'm proud of you."

Seems like she waited all day for her work to be recognized.

As a human, I should identify with the predator, but I usually feel sorry for the prey. I admire a cat's hunting skills, but I'm squeamish about the result. That has never made sense, but in an ongoing survey of my own design, I find that I am far from alone. Let me gather up the bug remains in some old newspaper.

"Ready to go outside? You can wander around while I find a suitable place to bury the cricket."

The western light is warming our bit of lawn and the wind off the pond has calmed. A good-sized evergreen about fifteen feet out and a few shrubs close to the foundation provide Miss Kitty with plenty of areas to explore. She moves around the tree with such focused intent that I almost expect a rabbit to jump out and take off running. With her head permanently cocked to one side, she would probably fall over if she tried to pursue anything. After a careful examination of the large pine tree, Miss Kitty throws herself onto the grass, belly up. I wouldn't think of offering her a tummy rub now. She's on her own. This is her time to enjoy all the sensations of the earth, smells and sounds I can mostly only imagine with my dull senses. She probably knows all about the insect life going on beneath the grass. Such comparisons help to keep me humble. In any case, we share the warmth of the sun and the stillness of the late afternoon air.

"Miss Kitty, I'm going to bury the cricket remains under this pine tree. This mulch comes in handy for so many things, mostly for relocating earthworms in trouble. You don't care. You never go after worms. What would be the challenge?" I've said it before- if God is an earthworm, I'm in. I'm lifting up a couple of inches of this stuff to find marvelous soil beneath. No, it isn't really a marvel, just great soil brought in by the truckload long ago to cover up the heartless clay that lets almost nothing of interest grow.

I actually have saved a great number of earthworms. You've got to figure a little worm deserves a chance if you see him on a winter's morning with snow on his back, but only half frozen, inching across the sidewalk. A puff of warm breath and a little warm spit will bring him right back. Tuck him under a few inches of mulch and he should be fine. I think of earthworms as I do of ants. They have dreadfully low status, and yet the Earth could not go on without them.

"Where are you going? I'm watching you, my dear. If you disappear, I'll have no choice but to skip town and leave no forwarding." I've never had to tell an owner that I've lost track of their pet, and I don't ever want to have to.

New clients have told me stories about calls they've received while vacationing. People who had agreed to care for their pets - not pet sitters- had let the pets get away from them somehow or thought they had. There must be endless versions of such calls, every one of them appalling. I listen to them as a professional pet sitter, but also as a pet steward. The person responsible in these stories always did something really stupid, not surprisingly since it was usually Bubblehead Neighbor Kid or Crazy Uncle Fred.

I always listen, imagining my vacation mood destroyed by a call from one of the above mentioned underqualified persons. I might hear that my dog was accidentally left out in the fenced yard all day, so he dug his way out and hasn't been seen since. Or that my cat has simply disappeared, even though BNK (see above) or CUF (ditto) has ransacked the house looking for her, loudly calling her name. I won't glorify any stories by relating them here. That's a book by itself, and best written by Stephen King.

Yes, I've talked about pets on the loose already. Here's why I'm circling back to it. My first and most important responsibility as a professional pet sitter is to manage the whereabouts of the pets I'm caring for. No one paying for my services should have a moment of worry. Did I ever have a close call? Oh, yeah.

One Christmas morning, about 6:45, following her human's instructions, I put a little Chihuahua /terrier mix on her tie-out just beyond the front porch steps. She was a sweet little dog and quite the lady, unable to relieve herself if anyone was watching. I would spy on her through the lace curtains to make sure she was focusing on her task (hey! my mother taught me a few things). She would then come in for breakfast before we took a short walk. That's how it was supposed to go, and so it had for several days running.

It was a dreamy, almost spiritual morning, with large, soft snow-globe flakes covering everything, in the first snow of the season. I was mesmerized. The world was quiet and there was no traffic. Snow like that makes everything glitter. Imagine my amazement when I peeked through the lace to see – WHAT? – the tie-out with a cute little red collar on the end. Little Miss ChiChi had gone on her own walkabout.

Panic, it seems, is where raw disbelief meets a screaming sense of urgency. I didn't remember opening the door and dashing out, but I seemed to come to my senses about halfway down the block. As a practical person, I always look for a strong point to work from, and I realized I was already there. The surface of the fluffy new snow was unbroken except for Miss ChiChi's footprints and I was following them. Snow was still falling lightly but steadily, and gradually covering those prints. I believed I was gaining on her, although she wasn't in sight. In the next block, the increasingly faint prints veered to the left, going up a driveway and through a gate. My heart was pounding as I ran into the fenced yard, closing the gate behind me. In the diagonal corner stood a bewildered Miss ChiChi.

I recall saying something such as, "What's wrong, sweet thing? Did you run out of real estate? Come on. Let's go home."

I knelt and smiled. She had to be getting cold. She ran to me and I scooped her up. She weighed no more than five pounds, but it wouldn't have mattered. With my adrenalin pumping, I could have hauled a retriever over my shoulder.

I gave her the lecture. "You can't know this, but if I hadn't found you, I'd have had to leave town. You just don't know how important you are, you cute little dickens." Miss ChiChi wasn't going to tell about her adventure, and I was tempted not to. The owners would need to know, and perhaps invest in a Houdini-proof harness. That little dog followed the same script as most dogs do. The longer the family is away, the more inclined their dogs are to go looking for them. Besides, every dog knows that romping in that first snow of the season is irresistible.

"Well, hello, Miss Kitty. Are you ready to go in? Oh, sure, flop over. Here's your last tummy rub of the day. You won't have many more warm evenings, either, my dear, but that's another thing you already knew." She lazily extends one foreleg, then extends her claws to their full length. "I can see we still have work to do in the morning. Look at those monster claws." Why have I never thought of bringing the clippers outside? A challenge for tomorrow.

"Now we really are going in. Come on, sweetie." What a great cat, and she so reflects the kind of person she lives with. Friendly without being sentimental. Strong, smart, and no-nonsense. We make much of how often dog owners and their dogs resemble one another, and I think a more subtle resemblance exists between cats and their humans. With dogs, it's physical, for dogs can vary so much in their appearance. With cats, it's all in the attitude.

"You hardly ate any of your food from this morning. Busy playing with the cricket, right? Maybe you'll have an appetite later. Goodbye, Miss Kitty. I'll see you in the morning. I love you."

We've got to go back to the house to pick up Maggie. She loves the Morgan Street reservoir and it's too isolated for walking her out there after dark. It's just 5:15. Perfect. These lightly scheduled days when everything goes as planned are heavenly. Not that I could stand everything being normal all the time.

Miss Kitty is the kind of cat anyone could love, never a moment's problem for her human. My cats are loveable, but from time to time I've had a quirky one. I keep a four-foot cage in the dining room for Shadow. He goes into "rehab" a few times a year. He manages to be perfectly normal for about six to eight months, then he begins to urinate randomly. His mother taught him not to use a pan. He will use one if he's caged, so he lives in the cage for a couple of weeks to get his mind right. When he comes out he's fine for quite a while. I'm just glad to know the source of his confusion.

Where's my car? I seem to say that a lot. Here we are. I like this time of day in Oberlin. There's nobody around so getting home takes about a minute.

Undesirable behaviors in pets often have a medical basis. If you can eliminate medical reasons, then it's behavioral. You have to educate yourself about what the pet needs. Not to worry – your pet will help you. Animals can become habituated to those unwanted behaviors because they usually will have hidden the problem for a long time before they start acting out. Once you make some favorable changes, your pet may very well not change immediately. Give him time. Maybe more changes are required. Know that when someone of a different species is living with you, you are forever not just a loving steward of that creature but also a student of his ways.

CHAPTER 13

5:20 Maggie's walk

I really am going to get a bicycle for the kind of trip I just took. Let's go in and get our girl.

"Maggie! Hi, sweetheart! Oh, wagga wagga. Are you ready to go to Morgan Street? Yep, Morgan Street! You just got a lot of beauty rest. Oh, yes, it did you a lot of good, too. You are beautiful. Let's get your leash." We always use a leash on public walkabouts. It's the law, and I like it that way.

"Okay. Jump in. Let's get your seat belt situated." Took me forever to find one that gave her the freedom to sit or lie down. Designers of these things must be thinking of dogs that take short trips, not like my girl. She's been known to log some serious sleep time in the back seat. As for me, I'm still learning to remember the darn thing.

And here we go.

I never put a leash on Maggie until we get to wherever we're walking. Actually, I have complete control over her in the yard because of an understanding we have. She knows her boundaries, so that's no problem. At times, she tests whether I'm willing to drop everything while she takes her time rolling around in the grass. No one loves grass and sunshine more than Maggie. Although she realizes I'm waiting for her and holding the car door open, no amount of begging, pleading or fierce commands will bring her out of a seeming reverie. But when I say, "I'm going to get your leash" she pops up and comes running. Apparently being tethered in her own yard is humiliating. Whatever works. Know your pet.

Okay, we're turning onto Cedar Street. This is such a pretty part of town. We pass Victorians, bungalows, and architectural mutts. Every single house has its own charm. People park on the street because most old houses here lack garages (if you want people talking about you in this town, try building a garage. Everyone will hash over what a snob you've become). The street is narrow, made almost into a single lane by the on-street parking, giving me the feeling of sneaking up on Morgan Street by an alleyway.

"Hey, good girl, you ready for Morgan Street?" I like to reach back and touch her paws. She actually doesn't like it at all, and almost always withdraws her paws. She then sniffs and kisses my hand. Just a ritual. It's such a treat to walk with Maggie on an easy day like this. We can – correction – will take our time, going at Maggie's pace. Sometimes my schedule is such that I have a cluster of stops between 3:00 and 6:00 for dogs whose owners work long days. I may also have to turn right around and start putting pets to bed whose owners are out of town. I don't usually work much past 8:30 at night, because when clients' pets are home alone in a quiet house, they go to bed early. Tonight, except for putting

Popcorn to bed, I can enjoy my own pets and catch up on call-backs.

Looks like we may have the place to ourselves. "Come on, baby, jump out. That's my girl."

Sometimes we see dogs joyfully swimming in the Morgan Street reservoir. Maggie averts her eyes. I've seen her jump or dash away when accidentally stepping in puddles or on grass that obscured standing water. She has muscled me off of sidewalks to avoid puddles. At such times I remember the duck hunter who was trying to lure her from the back of the whelping box when she was a pup. She would have ended up in the pound, for the best trainer in the world could not have made her do the very thing her breed is known for. Yes, she's a smart and beautiful dog, and a true Labrador in disposition, but those webbed feet, the oily coat and the powerful upper body of a swimmer will forever remain unused assets.

"Come on, pokey, let's get out to the actual reservoir." The short gravel driveway leading to the water is the only such surface Maggie encounters. It doesn't seem to hurt her feet, but something about it makes her walk in a plodding, thoughtful way. Because so many dogs walk in this area, this may just be a heady sensory experience. Maybe the surface has nothing to with it. All that I love about this place is that Maggie loves it. It is, otherwise, just a narrow muddy path through tall weeds on the rim of a mostly abandoned old reservoir.

"Come on, honey bun, off to the right. We have always gone counter clockwise and I suppose we always will.

No changes for us." I don't know the average number of dogs and people who go around on this path each day, but Maggie knows. This is her evening newspaper. She keeps close tabs as only she can on who has been here and when. She may know a bit about wherever they'd been before, too. Me? I just know it's a great time to share with my dog.

While Maggie's senses keep her grounded in the here and now, my indelible memories of this place connect me to old loves, long-lost friends, and the quirky aspects of this little town. Someday my memories of these walks will be a bittersweet part of that mental tableau.

The fishermen we occasionally encounter have told me that the city stocks the reservoir with bluegill. If one of those fellows sits out in the sun too long, he may see a huge fish, always at least three feet long in the breathless re-telling of it. No one ever catches much, as far as I know. Maggie loves smelling the gear, the bait, the beer and the lunches. She might have been fascinated by the swans that used to live here, but she would merely have stood gazing at them, along with me. It is said that the city re-homed them when it became too much trouble to move them temporarily for the July 4th celebrations. We lost a bit of our façade of gentility when that happened, whatever the real reason was for their leaving us.

"Maggie, let's keep moving. They'll get us for loitering one day." Honestly. I could grow roots.

In the misty long ago, a young auburn haired woman used to sit on these banks, fishing with a young sandy-haired man. She loved those sandy curls and that funny artist /

teacher who was a dead ringer for Dr. Demento. She loved him so much, she smoked his cigarettes just to keep him from smoking. Imagine that. Who would be so romantically selfless, so foolish? Yep. But no more. The only creature I'd lay my life down for now is my dog. That's what life can do – teach you lessons you didn't ask for but probably needed to learn.

By the way, I wouldn't do that for a cat because any cat worth her salt wouldn't need my protection.

"What is so darned fascinating here, now? Some people are coming, Mag. Move over. Good girl."

The path is narrow, with a steep slope on both sides. There's no way to go but down, and fast. One day Maggie was conducting one of her detailed examinations of the cattails or maybe it was sedge. Or purple loosestrife? Someone needs to yank that stuff out. At any rate, some canine urine signature was so intriguing, Maggie stepped down too far to get a better fix on it. She slid into the water. My first move – and a stupid one- was to pull up on the leash. She behaved as any animal would with something pulling up on her neck. She made that circular movement with her head, trying unsuccessfully to get out of her collar. By now, she was in a spot that was not sloping, but straight down. Nothing offered itself as a means for her to get a foothold up, or for me to step down closer to her. Her look of panic made me decide to slide in with her. If she was going to drown, I would drown, too, trying to help her. I was surprised in retrospect to realize that she had no idea of how to keep herself afloat, let alone swim. She is a purebred

Lab, for Pete's sake. My left foot luckily came down on a small rocky ledge a few feet below the murky water and I used it as leverage to lift her up and shove her back onto the path. I managed to crawl up, grabbing at tree roots and getting mud down the front of myself. We stood on the path regarding each other, trying to calm down, both dripping wet and stinking of Old Reservoir, something Maggie didn't mind at all. Shaking herself off seemed to be all she needed to recover completely. I took a bit longer, but I soon began to regain my sense of playfulness. We passed a few people out for a stroll, and I enjoyed offering them a genteel "hello" as they gave us both wondering stares.

"Come on, Mag. We're on the home stretch. Oh, here comes a pretty dog. Ooh! Another Lab. Take it easy." A woman being pulled along by a handful.

"Hello. Beautiful black Lab. Is it okay if Maggie says hi?"

"Oh, of course. Be careful. Our girl is just a year old and quite the jumper. Your chocolate is pretty, too, and so well behaved."

"Maggie is a grown-up. It takes a while. Time and training and lots of patience."

"We've almost given up that she'll ever be any different."

"I remember that stage, too. I had the advantage of having worked in blind rehab, and I had enough experience with Labs trained to be marvelous dog guides. So I knew what Maggie could do, even though she acted like a raving nut most of the first year or so. Just be consistent, and one day she'll surprise you. It turns out they're listening, but they just can't be bothered until they're ready."

"Oh? You're right about one thing. It will be a surprise. And the sad thing is, my husband is looking for any excuse to get rid of her. But thanks."

"Say goodbye, Mag. Oh, you liked her, didn't you?" She recognizes a kinship with other Labs. That tail really gets a workout. I hope that woman doesn't give up. "Thanks for being on your best behavior, girl of mine. You showed that lady what she'll have if she works for it." Darn it, I forgot to give her my card. Somehow when I talk too much I manage to forget the important stuff.

"Now what? Hey! No food wrappers, piggy. Ooh, and what's this lump...yuck. Give it. Give it. Good girl." So close to suppertime, that release could not have been easy. Dogs are scavengers. That's that.

"Here's our car, Mag. Let's get you home to a meal that isn't moldy or fly-covered. But, hey, that's just my quirky idea of what's good for you. Jump in. That's my girl."

Thanks to the great British dog trainer Barbara Woodhouse, I was able to teach Maggie when she was a pup, not just to "give," but to let me reach down her throat if necessary. Now she drops the stuff I disapprove of, and opens wide for my help when she's choking.

Okay, let's make a left on South Main and get home. "You hungry, Mag? Dinner?" Oh, yeah. That's excitement. That's one of her words. I use the word "supper" for my own evening meal, so her meals have their own word. Less confusion. Both of her meals are "dinner." A client I love and admire was surprised that I taught Maggie any word at all for her meals. Why bother, she wanted to know. She said that when she set her dog's food bowl down, the dog knew it was time to eat. No argument there. Here's the difference. When I say "dinner" to Maggie, she gets really excited, whether the food has yet materialized or not. We're sharing the thought. That's as close to conversation as we're going to get. Just as when I say "Morgan Street," and she starts wagging her tail wildly, even if we're on the other side of the county. Same thing. Lots of fun. And I have not found the limits of how many words or phrases she can learn.

I'm snagged back on what that woman at the reservoir said about her husband looking "for any excuse to get rid of" their Lab. Another tragedy in the making. When people are part of a couple, or configure a household of any kind for that matter, some discussion before pet acquisition has to take place. Shoot, I wish I could have had that chat with the cats before I brought Maggie home. Everything changes, including life for pets already part of the household.

Confession time. Here's what I did many years ago, when I was still young enough to believe that some man someday would love me. Well, before that even. Remember Mr. Curly Hair, the guy whose cigarettes I smoked? He wasn't the bad guy in this. He was the good guy. One spring night he and I were walking home and we began to hear a kitten's cries in the distance. We ignored it for a while, and then stopped to listen. When we did, she appeared. She was a sparkling marmalade fluff ball. Mr. Curly Hair cleverly (and I thought wisely) said, "If she follows us all the way home, we'll keep her. Just don't pick her up. She probably already has a home."

I was still inexperienced about animals, but I realize now that Brandy had chosen us. She followed us all the way home and planted roots deeply in our hearts. She was smart, funny, daringly athletic and loving. I typically ran the vacuum with her in my arms, her paws around my neck. Brandy trusted me completely. When I didn't feel well, or on nights when I cried myself to sleep, she would fall asleep with her paw on my face. She enjoyed our parties, our friends, and our other cats. She grew into a beautiful slender girl with a bushy squirrely tail and a heart-shaped face. She had a way of vocalizing that sounded like a hybrid of meowing and human speech. In dreams, I understood that language.

Mr. Curly Hair and I didn't stay together, and I was granted custody of the cats. By the time the next man came along, Brandy and I were alone together. If I'd had any sense, I would have known that that was more than enough. But, no. This man claimed that we could have a much more solid relationship if I re-homed Brandy. That was all so long ago, I hardly recognize the young woman who thought that made sense. But I found someone to take her, someone whom I knew as a cat lover. I found out much later, and by default, that Brandy was miserable and took off eventually to re-home herself.

The man who pressed me to part with her turned out to be a heel who wasn't through testing me to see what I would sacrifice to gain his approval. Brandy was lost to me for no good reason. She chose me, and I betrayed her. I have never forgiven myself, and all these years later she haunts both my dreams and waking thoughts.

I hear similar stories from others. It isn't a gender issue. Women can play the same vicious game —"If you love me, you will (fill in the sacrifice of your choice). Such destructive nonsense.

Sometimes it isn't so nasty. Some people are simply not interested in sharing their homes with non-humans. That's perfectly fine. I happen to believe that people who like animals and people who don't are significantly different from each other. The distinction is not trivial. An attempt at a relationship between these two different kinds of people sooner or later may involve wheedling, begging, resisting, seething resentment and other forms of unnecessary suffering on both sides. Ultimately most of the suffering will probably be experienced by the pet that was never truly welcome. Pet stewardship can divide or unite people, just as surely as different values and views with respect to children, money and religion. 'Nuf said.

CHAPTER 14

6:10 Home for Supper

"Maggie, we made it. Let's go feed the kitties. Ready for dinner?" Ha! There goes that tail. And Cujo and Kiki are waiting to go in. "Come on in, you love birds."

"Hey, Herbie!" My second dog, no? He loves to meet me at the door, even when he isn't angling to get out. "Come here, sweet kitty. Let me pick you up." I just love those googly eyes.

That's the great thing about cats – not that there aren't lots of great things about cats – I love the ones you can pick up and cuddle with, and I love the ones who let you know they can't be bothered with you. So unlike the slavering loyalty of most dogs. A cat is not necessarily loyal, and his love and respect must be earned every day.

When I was a kid, the neighbors had a reject dog that lived on the end of a chain in a clearing, past the field that nearly surrounded their house. An old rusty barrel was his shelter in winter, and an old apple tree on the property line gave Charlie shade in the summer. His short yips always alerted my mother that he needed food and water. She would send me to fill his bowls and to give him a reassuring pat. His black furry coat – I think he was a poodle –was hopelessly matted. About twice a year Charlie would break his chain and take off down the road. We kids and many adult neighbors would go out to the road and yell encouragement. "Go, Charlie, go!" Even my staid evangelical mother would come running out of the house, wiping her hands on a dish towel, and join in, looking almost joyful. She would shout, "Run, honey! Keep going!" We hoped he would run off into the sunset and find a loving home. Rescue groups were virtually nonexistent and a trip to the dog pound would have meant euthanasia. The little nitwit always came right back, panting and wagging his tail, looking quite pleased with himself. Charlie needed some of that feline discrimination, but blind loyalty sealed his fate as a faithful dog.

"Herbie, let's set you down and put some supper together. We have a few callbacks to make, too, and I know you'll want to help me with those." Herbie's caterwauling while I'm on the phone is just as loud any time of day. Many people who have heard Herbie in the background have asked whether I had a parrot.

"Chopped chicken livers anyone?" And here goes the phone. Let me start distributing these while I catch that.

"Hello?...Yes, it is. Yes, since '91…. Yes, I take care of birds, too. You seem to know a lot about the service….Oh, Mary's bird shop, of course. She's a great woman……Yes, the fee per visit is based on a half hour of care, but I would have to see your situation. If you have an aviary, plus two dogs and three cats? A run-through would be necessary, so

I could give you a realistic quote. ..Well, no, if you decide not to use the service, I wouldn't want you to call me back..... No, seriously, there's no need...Why? Let me pose this to you. When you wake up tomorrow morning, you notice that none of the plumbing in your house is leaking and the toilet isn't running. Would you get into the phone book and call a plumber and tell him not to come over?....Good. Contact me only if you need me, and I hope you will. Thank you. I'm so glad you called. Bye."

My inner plumber is one of my best friends. It's part of the education of the public. When I'm crazy busy, I don't want people calling me to say they don't need me. You may think that sounds cold, but people who actually think that way are usually looking for a friend. Sometimes they imagine me as someone with nothing to do. They want to talk for hours about their pets. I understand that. Shoot, I can do that, too. What is hard for people to grasp is that I've turned my interest into a business. I am a business owner who loves animals. I am not some kind of animal nut, cat lady or hoarder who is just waiting for the phone to ring. I sometimes suspect that some of those callers may be just that.

"Okay, my sweeties, watch out for my big feet. Let's put a little more chicken in each bowl. No pushing, Herbie."

When they finish that, I'll put down some dry food. ""Maggie, look at how pretty you sit in the doorway. You want some chicken livers? Some dry food, cheese, and applesauce on the side. Sound good? Mmm, chicken."

"Kiki, you'll do better if you don't run from plate to plate." See? Just like people. That little calico will never learn. Life on the street makes hunger their life-long demon, even when they finally find a stable situation.

I love these elevated bowls for Maggie. How long did it take us to realize this had to be more comfortable than reaching down to the floor? She sits so patiently, waiting for her release word. "Okay." Oh, that enthusiasm, as if she never had this before.

Let me see what veggies I have for myself. Sometimes I have grand ideas of actually cooking a full-fledged meal, but that almost never happens anymore. I think I've forgotten how to cook most things. I'll bread and sauté that eggplant while I'm on the phone and maybe make a salad. Lettuce, olives, red onion, green pepper, and a lemon for the dressing. Perfect.

"Maggie, let's get you on the dining room side again, and we'll put up the baby gate until the cats have finished their meal. Love you." Baby gates are nearly a must for households with both dogs and cats, and this way I can cook and talk on the phone and not have to keep an eye on Maggie.

Knife, flour, egg and milk, and breadcrumbs, skillet. Now, can I read my own writing? Here we go. "Hello? Yes, this is Diana Carter, the pet sitter. You left a message for me earlier. You have the new puppy, right?....Ah, good decision. You'll both be staying home? I'm impressed.... Yes, we can meet. When would you like to do that?....How about Saturday at around 11:00?.... Perfect. I look forward to meeting all three of you."

Sometimes people listen. Breathtaking. They just want to meet me, so the puppy has a dog walker when he's old enough. These people say they sometimes work very long days. I've taken care of many dogs in their first year, just until their bladders are large enough to get them through the day.

Skillet's not too hot, just right. Here we go. Ooh, nice sizzle. I used to fry up the entire eggplant and stuff myself. Now I eat about half of it, with a salad and some cottage cheese on the side. I no longer eat as though I'm in a contest to see how much I can eat and still fit into my jeans. Don't get me wrong. There will always be two pieces of pie in the morning.

"Hello? Is this Karen? Great – hey, listen, I wasn't sure about your message. You were calling for someone else? ....You're a concierge? Ah, I see.... Where is the condo complex?.... West Side. I would love to help you, but I don't cover that area....Oh, you called who?....Yes, I hear she's very good...Three days and no callback....Gosh, I have no idea. Probably really busy, and if she's like me, she's a one-woman show. Don't give up on her. In fact, call her again... .I'm the only pet sitter who's called you back? Ha! I nearly always call everyone back, but at peak times I have had to be selective. ....Return the favor? But I haven't done anything. Just keep my name and number and give it out sometime. You sound diligent. Here's a suggestion - try thinking like a pet sitter. I suggest contacting groomers and vets. Find out what sitters they know the best. Maybe they know someone who would love to work one cluster of buildings full of pampered dogs, maybe someone just starting out and not on your radar. Those sitters are out there, but you won't find them by calling individual sitters...my mailing address? Oh, I learned never to give that out. People used to tie their unwanted pets to my yard light. Thanks for your interest.... You bet...Bye now."

Sounds a bit desperate. What pet sitter wouldn't love between six and ten clients within jogging distance of one another? Too bad it's so far away. I'm always working on good will. Just not sure it's always going to lead to something. Can't afford to do otherwise, though. I think of it like rain drops on a waxed car hood. Lots of isolated drops for a while, then with enough volume, they start running together.

This eggplant has browned beautifully. I have an end-of-season tomato, which I will lovingly slice. Maybe some cottage cheese and it looks like supper. I'm too tired to put a salad together.

"Hey!" Oh, boy, a kitty kerfuffle. Silky and Shadow are getting on each other's nerves, so Silky slaps Shadow. I won't intervene. That's not wise. The cats understand one another, or soon will. If the disagreement is intense enough, Sammy jumps in. He's top cat, although reluctantly. There they go, over the baby gate, not chasing each other, but running from Sammy. Now watch this – focus on the top edge of the baby gate. When I see it, I can hardly believe it myself. Sammy streaks across the kitchen, and goes over the baby gate. Watch – at the top of the arc –see it? – he hesitates. I suppose that that isn't possible, but he does it anyway, every time. Stop action! Call me crazy, but there it was, just now, once again. He stops, for just one long second, with a purposeful look on his face, at the exact middle of the arc, almost as if he's willing himself to hang suspended there. Magic, right here in my kitchen.

Sammy will catch one cat first – yep, he just caught Shadow halfway through the dining room and slapped him in the chops. Now he'll go find Silky. She is lightning fast, and by the time he catches up with her, he'll just give her a dirty look. Sammy's never been comfortable as the enforcer anyway, but he manages to get his point across.

Some cat people would try to intervene. I believe that's usually a bad idea. Cats have a pecking order, and even a kind of politics, involving status, resources, and real estate. My cats even seem to have a schedule for litter pan usage. Yep, the politics of potty breaks. They give each other threatening stares and paw whacks from time to time, but most communication is subtle – movements of the tail, ears, or head, for example. People have written books about body language, but we are amateurs when compared to the animal world. They not only communicate effectively by "reading" one another, but they read us, too. When you get out the carrier to take Schnookums to the vet, and realize that she has already found perfect safety behind the furnace, don't imagine she's psychic. You just revealed your intentions to her in countless physical ways.

By the way, don't bother trying to spell things either. That only works for a little while. Long ago Maggie learned "B-A-T-H." Spell it out and she would slink off into oblivion. Say the word "bath" outright and she had no idea what I was talking about. So much for outsmarting my dog.

Okay, food on plate. Let's try this. Oh, yeah, eggplant needs oodles of salt. "Hi, Maggie. Sure, we'll take the baby gate down. Oh, what's this? You're going to bow? Well, and right back at ya." She brings her front end down in a bow. As long as I reciprocate, she keeps bowing. I wonder if we look like two Japanese people not sure of our relative social status. We just keep bowing so neither of us will be the last one. "And again? Okay." I did not teach her this. "One more? Of course, my dear." She honored the horses this way, as I've told you. "Okay, Maggie, this is it. I'll let you have the last bow, and only because we have to stop sometime. Oh, yes, I love you so. Here's a hug." I've read in books how to teach your dog to bow, but Maggie actually taught me before I had ever heard of it. More magic. I am truly blessed.

Cottage cheese is good, mmm, another bite of eggplant. Getting a mouthful of food is a sure way to get the phone to ring. Honest. Hey! See there? "Hello?.... Yes, how are you?.... Are the kitties okay?....Sorry for chewing in your ear....Yep, you know me by now. I have you on the schedule for this weekend....So I should start in the afternoon, instead of first thing?....Let me make a note....I'm glad you called. I'll take good care of them ....Yes, I'll watch the front porch for deliveries..... Aw, that's sweet of you to say. And you're a marvelous cat mom, so I have to uphold the standard they're accustomed to. By the way, are you going to have workers in the house this time?.... Remember the guy with the big pipe wrench?...Yes, I know he was a plumber, but I didn't know he was going to be there. I really don't like surprises.... Great, so I'll expect a quiet house. Have a great trip....Right. Bye now." It's perfectly logical to have the bathroom remodeled while you're out of town. Just remember to tell me about it.

See? That's how it always works. If clients get me on the first ring, they know I'm eating something and they just have to brace themselves. A pet sitter's life is unlike any other. Eating while standing at the kitchen counter, drinking cold coffee in the morning, talking to myself most of the time, all the while surrounded by the endless beauty and mystery of the animals. It isn't for everyone, but I wouldn't change a thing. Okay, one more bite, and then I want to tour the garden before it's too late. It's almost 7:00. Can't forget the clippers.

"Hey, Maggie, let's go out." Ah, my ready companion.

CHAPTER 15

7:00 The Garden

All sorts of plants grow up around the house that would be unacceptable in suburbia. Along the porch I've always encouraged honeysuckle. Supposedly an invasive vine, this one is a perfect lady, climbing up the same trellis for years without so much as a straying tendril. Its fragrance in spring is like nothing else, sweet and light but oddly complex in the damp evening air. In the same garden are stonecrop and wild ginger. Once in a while, a Jack in the Pulpit shows up. Moving back toward the garden, around what may be the town's biggest black walnut tree, is pokeweed. The wildlife love its deep purple berries, so I've learned to tolerate this truly invasive plant. I have to thin out the purple-stemmed sprouts coming up everywhere in the spring. The black walnut, about ten feet around at the base and with a spread that shades the center third of the yard, makes the soil around it impossible for civilized gardening. I allow Mother Nature to do what she will, and she wills pokeweed.

"Maggie, what is it? A rabbit? Look all you want." Now I just have to make sure she doesn't eat the droppings.

We'll come back here to the barn, a structure that pre-dates the American Civil War, according to the original handwritten deed. Around it grows small clusters of heal-all, which Dr. Jones always claimed was an ironic name. He said that it was one of the few plants for which there was no use. I happen to love the shape of the seed pods, and clip them for dried arrangements, along with curly dock, timothy, and peppergrass. I have seen milkweed growing in the swale along the property line. I don't touch it, but in fact consider it a blessing. Solitary stalks of mullein always show up somewhere, never in the same place, apparently because the plant is a heavy feeder.

Red osier dogwood grows on its own, and it is almost customary around here to let it come up on property lines as a hedge. Hummingbirds love the blossoms. Along with it one may find the unattractive and unpleasant common buckthorn. Talk about invasive. I chop that out wherever I find it.

Why do I care so much about the outdoors? Walking dogs, I'm in it a lot. I've always been more comfortable being outside, grew up in the country, as I've mentioned. Some days I spend lolling around with clients' spoiled indoor cats, but many days I'm out in horizontal snow or rain with dogs. When I'm in tune with what's going on out here, I feel as though I'm living fully in the world. I can't be cooped up, and that's another reason pet sitting suits me.

So here we are in September, when the days are noticeably shorter. In other seasons, I long for autumn, to experience its serious and stimulating beauty. I've lived long enough now for autumn to suit me. Most of my life, the cool streams of air threading through sun-warmed days felt mysterious and somewhat unsettling. Now when I come to the garden in the evening to gather plants for drying I realize a sense of harmony. In earlier years, I though this time of my life would be scary. But now, in midlife, without the distractions of everyday life, standing here in the garden, I come home to who I am. I breathe in gladly all the sensations of this September evening.

The herb garden is good for me. My affection for the animal world can only stay healthy as long as I generate other interests to keep myself balanced. Maggie, sensing that I'm becoming inner-focused, always snoops around at a distance. "I have my eye on you, rascal."

My great-grandmother was Maggie Carter, who used herbs successfully to heal family members and neighbors in the late 19th and early 20th centuries. All eighteen of her children survived high fevers and various maladies because she knew how to turn herbs into poultices, infusions, teas, syrups, powders, decoctions, compresses, and baths. Good fortune surely played its part as well.

Sometime in mid-twentieth century many people, including the Carter girls, came to view that kind of folk knowledge as outmoded and turned away from herb-based remedies. I understand the instinct toward being modern, but I can't help feeling we ceded some power when we lost common knowledge of and respect for herbs. Why couldn't we retain traditions alongside the new developments? I don't think it has to be a case of "either/or."

I want to study herbs, both for myself and for my pets. Someday I may not be able to meet the physical demands of pet sitting, and perhaps I can turn this beautiful mess into another career. Yes, gardening is demanding, too, and my hands and knees are already a little the worse for wear, but they could rest in the winter.

If a genie were to appear right now and offer me the choice between more time in this world or a chance to travel back in time to correct mistakes, I'd take the time. As much as I could get. Mistakes? Oh, yes, I have made my share. And with each mistake, I've learned something about what I'm made of. I've made the big mistakes only once; to do otherwise would be to dishonor my own life. As the country boys like to say, there's no education in the second kick of the mule.

In business, in gardening and in life, I keep trying to trust the cycles that serve Mother Nature so well. In spite of all the browning and dying back at this time of year, she isn't getting ready to give up. She's investing in the future and taking a break. She drops seeds and spores, and then covers them all with enriching leaf mulch. She anticipates another go at it, after that obligatory and well deserved rest.

A couple of years ago, a sense of panic came over me briefly when I began to lose dogs from the roster at a fairly steady rate. I t wasn't an epidemic or a slump in the economy, but many dogs I had taken care of for a long time were dying of the effects of old age. The universe took a deep breath, paused, and then sent me more dogs. This cycle was one I had not anticipated, but I have learned that it is just as real as other kinds of economic cycles and as certain as the changing of the seasons.

I have said before that a small business like mine is either growing or changing (or both), or it is dying. It truly feels organic, a living thing. Remaining static bodes poorly for the long term.

My own life has seen periods of scary changes and the radical dying off of so much that I counted on. There have been times when it seemed there was no way out of trouble, and at the lowest point, that my life was over. In the dreary days before I started the business, I thought I had lost too much to start again. I was wrong. Somewhere within me were the resources to take another shot at it.

Years ago I had a friend whose religious training taught her that taking one's own life was a sin. My question to her was, how can we judge so severely someone in that much pain? Her answer was, it is wrong to second-guess God; that is, we can't know what God intends for our lives. I liked her answer. I think of that exchange sometimes when I consider how dramatically and how quickly my own life changed for the better. I don't know what made my life turn around, some spiritual force or my own pluck. But I do appreciate the part about not knowing what opportunities may lie around the corner.

So here's what's left of the garden. The hardier herbs I count on are oregano, parsley, and chives. Thyme is too dowdy and won't be invited back. I could try another variety, but I'm ready for something tall and colorful. Someday I'll have the luxury of time for experimentation. Chervil, which seems to be just another kind of parsley, died out on its own, or the rabbits ate it. Sweet Annie has its own section, and re-seeds itself. Its heavenly pungent fragrance should be against the law.

Oh, never mind. Except for the towering Sweet Annie, I've taken everything from the herb garden that can be dried. Right now I'm going to gather some of the outlying stuff that is part of nature's garden, not mine. Over here is four-feet tall curly dock, a plant that dries into a deep rust color. Let's get an armload of that, and then some velvetleaf. Its dried pods look like pies, so why wouldn't I like it? The leaves themselves don't dry well, so I'll knock those off later. The peppergrass, which is supposed to prefer poor soil, has gone gangbusters near the compost bin this year. I enjoy the tiny round seed pods that come out from the main stem. This plant is known as Poor-man's Pepper, but this poor girl has never had the nerve to try the seeds as a pepper substitute. I remember it as almost a ground cover when I was a child, but these plants are almost three feet high. The pale yellow bunch of them will contrast well with the curly dock.

"Maggie? Stay close, my girl." If I tether her, she howls as if she's being tortured. Sounds like a banshee with a sore rear end. I've never heard anything else like it, and I don't care to, so I just keep an eye on her.

Here on the east side of the yard is a shade garden and a bit of a pet cemetery. In early summer ferns, coral bells, and bleeding hearts liven this area surrounded by tall pines. Now the pines rule the day with no flirtatious blossoms to distract from them, and only the little stone markers provide interesting detail.

The great Carolyn Cat doesn't have a fancy marker with her dates, because I have no idea when she was born. I remember too well when that plain brown tabby with the notched ear died. In the last spring of her life, she succumbed to kidney failure. Although she was a long-time street cat before I took her in, she always showed a lot of class. When I came home on that sad day, I found her half in and half out of the cat pan. Carolyn had been experiencing projectile urination, and she used the last of her strength to keep from soiling the house.

Like so many pets, that ordinary looking tabby was a stand-out as my friend and as a citizen of the domestic and wild worlds she inhabited. I named her Carolyn as a quick way to infuse something pretty into her difficult life. I attached a pet door to the barn to give her ready access to shelter, and then I put food and water bowls just inside the barn entrance. Even after my anti-pet beau was long gone, I continued to see her as an outside cat. She lived that way for years.

"Outside cat." Yep, I just said that and I can't believe it myself. When I hear such a term these days, my head can snap around like that gal in "The Exorcist" or a very hungry owl. That phrase does not bring out my best reaction, but it is one true barometer showing how far I've come. And still learning, I hope.

Looking back, I see so clearly that her life was unceasingly perilous. Some dangers were closer to annoyances, but Carolyn battled some truly threatening foes.

Carolyn was a wise cat who, as far as I knew, never went anywhere near the street. She was not about to be road kill. The everyday dangers of the yard kept her busy. The least but most common of these was my feet. As any adoring cat will do, she parked herself as close to me as possible. When I was hanging out clothes or working in the garden, I was bound to step on her. She always forgave me, but only after a full-out attack on my calf muscles. She never learned to stay out of the way, but she taught me to watch my step. One afternoon, while bringing in laundry, I stepped on remains of her wildlife meal that was swarming with yellow jackets. Their stings were effective, as her scratches and bites had not been.

The other backyard danger was the lawnmower, at least as far as Carolyn was concerned. She was always in view, as I made the monotonous trips up and down the long back yard. She would perch on the hood of my car, squinting off into the distance as though some unseen threat just over the horizon was her real concern. She may have actually been worried about me, since she usually took off when the work was done.

Carolyn used the squinty eye routine in one other situation. For a time we had a neighborhood rooster, and he liked my yard more than some. I can't explain that. Carolyn, like any animal, knew how to evaluate her opponent, even one of another species. She despised the rooster and knew that she would be no match for his spurs and beak. She could watch him for hours through nearly closed eyes, pretending to gaze absently toward the horizon or fighting sleep. The rust-colored rooster strutted about like the king of all, taking over our yard whenever he pleased. He crowed randomly, although he did seem to enjoy sounding off in my ear just when I fell asleep on the porch with a book over my face. Carolyn always seemed perfectly controlled, right up until she wasn't. Gamblers might have had fun, betting on just when Carolyn would explode with fury, as she occasionally did, lunging after the rooster, hissing, clawing, her fur standing on end all the way out to the end of her tail. The rooster would be so startled that he would flutter into the air several feet, then land only to be faced with a still furious feline in close pursuit. He would make desperate clucking sounds as he dashed off across back yards to safety.

As much as Carolyn's dreams may have involved fresh chicken, the unfortunate bird sought refuge in the barn one bitter cold Super Bowl Sunday and was torn apart by an unknown predator.

.   Before I ever met her, my tough girl laid out ground rules for dogs. In those days, stray dogs could make life for homeowners miserable, trampling flower beds and getting into trash cans. I never had those problems. Dogs actually crossed the street to avoid her.

Carolyn's strongest reaction to danger involved a threat I never saw. The property to the east here has always remained wooded behind the house, although the line goes back as far as mine. Carolyn would often position herself between me and those woods. Sometimes she would slink toward the trees, growling low, her fur puffed out. Most of the time, I was mildly amused by it. No animal or deranged person ever materialized. I called her my "guard cat," and left it at that.

We had good times together. I would spend time with her at the end of every day, sitting with her on the porch, giving her tummy rubs. When I chopped wood on winter afternoons, Carolyn would take breaks from guarding me, stealing laps of my hot cocoa. She once showed me how she could emulate a possum when she got caught between a mother groundhog and her litter. I thought she had died from fright.

After she had lived outside for about ten years, I brought her inside. She was starting to look like a little old lady, with a potbellied physique and thinning fur. Life outside is hard, and she had lived far longer than most cats outdoors. Within about six months of living indoors, she was quite rejuvenated, with renewed strength and a beautiful body covered with a shiny coat. She lived like Cleopatra on her barge for another seven years, usually stretched out in front of a sunny window. She was the perfect feline companion.

Even in those days, it was kidney failure that brought down aging cats. When Carolyn's time came, she still did things her own way. She loved Dr. Bob, and put up with fluid therapy and the baths he gave her afterwards. She rubbed against him, purring loudly while he used a warm blow dryer on her fur. She flatly refused to eat the food he prescribed. She was, after all, a life-long hunter and had no tolerance for canned glop.

On the night before she died, Carolyn jumped on the bed and slept curled up against me, something she had never done before. The following afternoon, I pulled into the driveway to see a semi-circle of neighborhood strays holding vigil out near the barn. I knew she was gone.

I made some major mistakes with Carolyn. Not only was I a complete dunce for not bringing her in when I first met her, but at the end of her life, I couldn't let her go. I couldn't let my selfishness dissolve into decency, so she died alone on the cellar floor. She should have died in my arms.

The day after she passed, anyone might have seen a sobbing woman digging a little grave among the pines. That woman was recognizing she was burying a piece of her own heart. She was parting with a fine teacher and a true friend. She was saying goodbye to the only creature who had ever had an interest in protecting her.

I could have sworn that I heard her meowing under the front windows for a day or two after she was gone. As if that weren't irrational enough, I actually went out looking for the meowing kitty. Some cats are more special than others, and Carolyn was one of the great ones.

"Hey, Maggie. Let's go in. We have callbacks to make and some dishes to wash. You can go with me later to put Popcorn to bed. What is it?" Oh, yes, Canada geese, and of course now I hear them. My girl loves things in flight. "C'mon, let's head for the house."

Maggie chased after birds and low-flying planes in earnest when she was a pup. Like me, she has now learned that many things are best enjoyed from a distance.

It was in this area just at the back corner of the house that Maggie made me understand inadvertent training. When she was about a year old, she had begun sleeping in my bed. At some point, she began to wake me at about 4:30 every morning. I assumed she had to pee, so we would march down the steps, through the house, and out the side door. She wasn't usually eager to urinate. One of my many training books suggested that walking dogs around in circles was a way to encourage them to pee. I tried this, and was quickly successful in getting Maggie to prance around in a circle. She would lift her feet just like a circus pony strutting her stuff under the big tent, and give me sidelong glances as if to say, "How am I doing?"

So I had become just another middle-aged woman, wearing a nightie, dew-sodden slippers and a disgusted expression, preparing her dog for show business. I needed just one more 4:30 wake-up call to correct this mess of my own making. The night came when I felt the familiar thud of Maggie's feet hitting the floor, and her wet nose on the back of my hand. "Maggie, go to bed." The wet nose touched me again. I remained still and used my sternest voice. "Go to bed." A few moments of silence and waiting paid off. Maggie jumped up on the bed and went back to sleep. Oh, so easy. Was that the end of it? Oh, no. The mutual training efforts of dogs and their humans are never over. She tested me a couple more times. Occasionally she really has to go out, but I don't stir until I feel a second and very insistent nudge on my hand.

Hey, it's funny now. Actually it was funny then, except for the soggy slippers. I didn't set out to get a dog to make me laugh, or to show me my shortcomings, or to teach me how to love. Thinking back, I set out to get a dog for protection. Right, and ended up with a Lab. Frankly, most of my life I've needed protection from my own foolishness, and the greatest dog in the world is not up to that task. No, instead I ended up with Maggie, who has never, as far as I can tell, sensed danger. She has so far snored peacefully through two break-ins.

She is a master of humor, from the subtle to the slapstick, and has made me laugh nearly every day. She is such an astute teacher that her lessons have sunken in painlessly and effectively. I am such a plodding, dull-witted student that I have recognized the improvements in myself well after the lessons were laid down. I don't know how else I would have learned that I didn't have to be serious all the time, or that mistakes are not the end of the world. I was thankful to discover that being consistent and clear is almost always useful, and that every time I feel certain of something, I need to question myself one more time. I acquired a healthy balance between pride and humility.

I used to pray that my heart would not freeze over, and Maggie more than took care of that tall order, too. I have learned to love Maggie more than my own life. I have learned not to feel self-conscious or overwhelmed in the brown-eyed gaze of someone who sees all the way through me but who loves me anyway.

"Okay, Mag, let's make some calls."

Ugh. I really don't like facing dirty dishes. They'll disappear while I'm on the phone, unless I have to hold Herbie while I'm talking.

"Hello, this is Diana Carter, the pet sitter. You left a message about taking care of your dog....Yes, I'm sure I'd be available. How did you hear about me?......I see, and what community do you live in?....Because I don't go everywhere.....Gotcha......And it's just the one dog? ......German shepherd mix? Who has taken care of her in the past?.......You are so right, it's a breed that is often protective. If she's protective of you, I'm fine. If protective of property, I'd never get in....Relatives and neighbors don't count. They share some of your scent, and there may be other aspects of continuity. I'd be somebody showing up in a car.......No, not at all. Here's what I do. We can meet soon to talk more about the service, and your dog and I can get acquainted. We need to get along with each other at that level first. Then we'd set up a day and time when I'd come over in your absence. We'll see if she lets me in, and the test is just that simple. Sound good? ....Great. Next Tuesday....what time were you thinking of? I have 10:15 or 2:30, unless you need evening. Okay, 10:15 it is. Let me get the address.....this gives us plenty of time before your trip in case you need to make other arrangements. I'm hoping it works out.... Wonderful. I'll see you Tuesday. Bye."

I got through all that without a peep from Herbie. Okay, now this one could be prickly. "Hey! Kiki, don't you dare soil my floor. Out, and you, too, Cujo. See you two later." That was close. Cujo is a great house guest, but his girlfriend is a tramp.

Here goes. I hope this lady is willing to listen. "Jan? It's Diana. I know you have questions about the note I left....Right, I'm sure Rhianna comes back to you when you're in the yard with her....Of course, she's yours. That's the difference. When I take care of a dog for more than a couple of days, she will always begin going farther and farther afield. She's looking for her family....They're pack animals. She doesn't do it when you're there because – well, because you're there....No, I'm not asking for anything drastic, but since you don't have a fenced yard, we need to do something. Do you have a leash for her? I haven't found one.... Oh, good, in the basement? Great! Maybe you could resurrect that for the time being ....Well, people use fenced yards, leashes, underground electronic fencing....I'd love to let her run free, too. There are some good options for that. Do some thinking and some pricing. See what works....If you don't do anything? Well, just leave the leash for now. But I can't be part of a situation where a beloved dog just wanders off....How likely? Very...Oh, no, Jan, I'm not threatening anything. The threat is Rhianna's own natural inclination to seek her pack, and we have to manage that....I know you love her. That's the challenge for all of us, understanding how they think, so they don't harm themselves in this crazy world we've created…..Good. Just think about it. Have a good evening. Bye."

I've got one more call that I have to make before it's too late, but we'll go see Poppy first. It's almost 8:00. Seeing that sweetheart will cheer me.

"Let's hit it, Maggie. One last time."

CHAPTER 16

8:00 – Poppy Goes to Bed

I have Poppy's nighttime ritual memorized. His human provided me with an instruction sheet, as many clients do, although I have an excellent memory for these things. I don't know why. I can still remember pets' routines and the layouts of clients' homes I haven't entered in years. Not the entire layout, mind you, but blindfolded I could find the pans, litter, can openers, pet food, leashes, and grooming supplies. I know why I don't remember anything else about the houses – I didn't care about anything else.

"Look, Maggie, at the funny lady walking her dog. You would love that. She has her arm fully extended, stumbling along on the balls of her feet, the leash wrapped several times around her right wrist. You'd drag her down to her knees, wouldn't you, sweetie?"

Where do people get the idea that wrapping the leash around the wrist is a good idea? The dog lurches after a squirrel, and the most wondrously articulated joint that woman has is suddenly, and I mean suddenly, in jeopardy. How foolish is that? Possible injuries aside, compromising the wrist is never wise. She looks so certain that she's doing it right. Let's hope she's on that always-improving, self-educating journey that I like to think I'm on.

This is the time of day when we can enjoy driving through town. The students at this college are so serious that most of them are already slouched over their books in the library, and will be there most of the night. And who knows what the townspeople do? I assume they drive into Cleveland on the weekends for something to do, and on weeknights like this they're comatose in front of the tube. This evening the square is one lovely, shady expanse with the occasional dog walker or window shopper.

An evening pet visit can be a dog's last trip out before bedtime, the medication of a cat, or the covering up of birds. It's a necessary part of the job, and the hardest for me. This is a beautiful evening, and the visit is just across town, so it's easy enough. Sometimes I've had to go quite a distance, and the weather may be less than ideal. There have been a few times when lousy winter weather was coming in, and I drove through horizontal snow to get to my little charges. Neighbors of clients have keys, usually, but I've always managed to get there. In the case of bad weather, I leave extra food and water, assuming I may not get there on time in the morning. The other negative aspect of night visits is expense. Quite often the visits are isolated in the appointment book. Those sparse trips are expensive, as compared to trips that are part of a full daytime itinerary.

Evening visits are exhausting, too, if they go on too long. My record for an unbroken string of nighttime visits is seventeen days. I didn't realize how tired I was during one pet care stretch until the client called me from Florida to say she would be a day late coming home. When I got off the phone, I started crying. I had a solid schedule from 7:00am until about 6:00pm, then I put her dogs to bed at around 9:00pm. I was home by 10:00. Sometimes I just need a break; nevertheless, I love what I do and stretches of long days are just part of the deal.

"Maggie, what are you crying about? Oh, my, it's the husky from our neighborhood. I've never seen those people walk their dog before. Hey, take it easy. I know you have a crush on him. Quiet! There, that's better."

She whimpers every time she sees that handsome devil, and he pays no attention to her. Spayed and neutered, they still know what they are. Let's park around the corner here on Cedar. "Okay, Mag, I'm going in. You be good. I'll be right back."

Not entirely true, of course. This may take about thirty minutes or so, just like all my visits. Poppy is so small and not in his cage, so I always go in assuming he could be right at the door, rather like Herbie the cat. I always go in quietly. "Poppy? Where are you, sweetie?" Hmm. Not in the living room. "Poppy?" Let's check the dining room and kitchen, but those aren't his favorite rooms in the evening. I'll just put his little plate in the sink and turn off the lights as I go. Can't forget this little bowl of spring water. "Hey! Pretty boy! Say something."

I'll start the evening ritual, and he's bound to show up. His toys come off of the bed and into his toy box. The quilt is littered with bird poo, the only clue that he pays any attention to these toys. Let me get this cleaned up.

"Poppy, are you here? Ah! Look who's sitting in the window. Have you been spying on the neighbors? Good boy. Well, you get to watch me close the place down, pretty bird."

"The lights are all off but in here, sweetheart. Want a drink? No? Last chance. Sure? Okay. Let me get your covers on the cage." If I don't do this just right the cage can tip over. The sheet is one thing, but she likes this heavier cover over him, too. "Here we go. Are you ready? Hop onto my finger. Good boy. Let's get you up on your roosting perch. There. You know this routine better than I do. Such a good little bird. Who wouldn't love you? I'm closing the covers over you and I want you to go to sleep. I'll turn this last light off and wait until you're quiet. Good night, sweet beast."

When I was a social worker, I met a new client who introduced me to her pet parakeet. She had inherited the bird from a friend who had passed about six months before. Rita, whose own activities had been somewhat curtailed by vision problems, was thrilled to have the bird. Her friend had taught him lots of phrases and complete songs with all the verses. What a great companion he would be! As she told me about him, he sat on his perch gazing at both of us. Such a pretty green and yellow creature, nearly a figurine, except for an occasional blink.

"Well, what has he been singing today?"

"That's what's so sad. Petie's been completely silent since I took him in."

"Broken heart? I've heard that birds bond strongly to ·one person."

"Maybe. I wonder whether I want to keep him. He's just an expense. I know it seems selfish, but I was hoping he would be a source of amusement, you know, and companionship. He was such a joy to my friend."

"Well, okay, how do you start your day, I mean what do you say first? Hello? Good morning?"

Rita shook her head. "Oh, no, I don't say anything."

"Nothing?"

"He's a talking bird. I'm waiting for him to say something."

Hmmm. "Maybe it doesn't work that way. My grandmother had a parakeet, and she always primed the pump in the morning by saying 'Good morning' several times and I don't remember what else."

"Oh, Diana, I'd feel so foolish, especially if he didn't say anything back."

So here I was, talking with a woman who was so depressed, she feared rejection from a fistful of feathers. "Let's try something. Do you remember what Petie said in his talking days? Or what he sang?"

"Well, he said, 'Hello, I love you, you're so pretty, gimme kiss. Other things, too."

"Good." I didn't mind looking foolish. I turned to the bird. "Hello, Petie. Hello. You're so pretty. Yes, you are. You're so pretty. Gimme kiss."

Petie's beak opened a bit, and he said, " Gimme kiss. I'm Petie."

We humans both suppressed our glee. Could we keep this going? Oh, not to worry. Now the challenge was going to be learning to ignore him while I conducted the interview I was there for. As we talked, Petie kept talking. Creating a monster had never been easier. Petie had just been waiting for permission! He went through the phrases we knew he could say, then he regaled us with proof of – one of my favorite phenomena- inadvertent training. He clearly said, "Oh, hell, where are my keys?" and "I need chocolate." When he really got going, he sang a bit of "The Java Jive."

Rita smiled. "I think he sings 'Happy Birthday' too."

Well, Rita called me weeks later to let me know that Petie was still talking and singing. He had revealed that he could sing "Itsy Bitsy Spider" and recite "Mary Had a Little Lamb."

As for Popcorn, he seems to have gone to sleep. I just wait until he stops making those soft chirping sounds, and that happens more readily than when I first knew him. It'll be okay to slip out now.

Every time I pass these hanging plants in the big front window, I think I hear them screaming. I'll water them tomorrow, even though I've never been asked to.

When I first got into the business, in anticipation of being expected to know everything, I bought *Stroud's Digest on the Diseases of Birds*. Robert Stroud was an internationally known ornithologist, made famous in the movie *The Birdman of Alcatraz*. Apparently a genius cursed with a flashpoint temper, he spent most of his life in prison for murdering two people. The book, still in print today, was published in 1939 when there were few vets, no antibiotics, and very little information about bird care available to the average person. Stroud was entirely self-educated, and developed a book that gave poultry farmers and hobbyist bird lovers a world of information. Many treatments for sick birds were concoctions made from ingredients found in everyone's kitchen. A fine avian vet has been a phone call away when I've needed him, and Stroud's book reminds me what a luxury that is. The book still makes a great read, beautifully written and packed full of still-relevant information.

Lock the front door, give it a jiggle. Poppy's locked in safe and sound. Even though this area is quite safe, the house itself seems to have an unsettling presence. I don't enjoy these evening visits.

"Hey, Maggie. Now if I were willing to spoil you the way you'd prefer, I'd take you through the junk-waffle drive-thru and get you some French fries. But I think I can spoil you without ruining your body chemistry. Let's go home and see what kind of doggie treats we have."

Back when I was still struggling financially, I sometimes ran out of dog biscuits. My bright idea was to take a few pieces of her kibble and sprinkle them with olive oil and

Italian herbs. I made a big deal about it and told her it was "Taliano." She thought she was getting the best treat in the world. Once in a while I still think of it and am gratified that she remembers "Taliano." She wags her tail wildly, curls her upper lip into a grin and prances around the kitchen floor in anticipation.

Look at that string of green lights all the way down Lorain Street. I won't make them all, even with no other cars to mess up my timing. I drive very defensively, in fact. With all the driving I do, I see a lot of people not driving very attentively, to say the least. All I have to do is remember the time I was laid off from a job with about a forty-five minute commute, and then suddenly found myself pulling into my own driveway. Not sure who was driving on that trip, but it wasn't the highly alert, sensible self I take so much pride in. These days, I just figure other drivers may have just gotten bad news from the boss, their doctor, their lawyer, or fill in the bogey man of your choice. Then they get behind the wheel and they're on the road with me. Don't get me started on all the other distractions. So I watch my driving and theirs.

"Okay, Maggie, we're home just in time for Katherine's dairy break. Jump out, sweetie. We'll let Cujo and Kiki in for a treat and then out. It's too late in the day for Kiki LeeKee to be living up to her name."

CHAPTER 17

8:30PM - Snacks and Grooming

A few years ago, Katherine Katz began to be a real nuisance at around 8:00 every evening. I would pick her up, only to be rewarded with arc-shaped scratches across my chest from her back claws. I would try brushing her, petting her, cooing at her, and ignoring her. Well, there are behaviorists who say we reward "bad" behavior in cats when we give them any attention. If I knew how long it took me to catch on, I'd tell you, but I don't. It was at least a year before I became so desperate that one night I said, "Hey, sweet girl, how about some cottage cheese?" Her huge eyes opened wide, as if some feline sense told her the two-legged one was no longer comatose. "Meow?" she asked. I headed for the kitchen with the beautiful white-faced tabby at my heels.

That was the beginning of the now- traditional evening dairy break. Depending on what their tummies can handle, they get cottage cheese, yogurt, or white cheddar cheese.

"Is everyone here? Where's Silky? Kitty-kitty-kitty! Aha! You weren't far. Let's get everything out of the fridge while I make one last call. Maggie, where do you belong?" Wonderful – she goes to the living room. Her treat comes later.

If anything ever happens to me, and someone adopts Maggie, they'll be amazed that whenever she hears someone say, "Where do you belong?" she runs to the middle of their living room. Think about it. What does your pet understand that is way outside the bounds of standard commands? Yep.

Oh, yes, one saucer for cottage cheese, three more for yogurt, and we'll sprinkle some chunks of cheddar on the big plate. "Easy, Herbie. Stick with the cheese." I swear he has a burgeoning allergy to dairy, so the cottage cheese is off limits. I don't have to watch them closely, for they must have figured out which treats suit their tummies. Except for Herbie. "Herbie. Right here, sweetheart. Good kitty."

Katherine Katz is an exceptional cat in that I actually know her birthday. Her mother was a neighborhood tramp who gave birth to four kittens on my porch during a rainstorm. I brought them all indoors and had my one and only experience of watching a litter's development and the mother's nurturing of them. I was present when Katherine opened her eyes for the first time and saw me. Her eyes and her ears were enormous, making her look like an adorable space alien. She looked at me, and finally she was gazing at me. She didn't blink for a long time, just watched me as I smiled and babbled at her. I realized I was quite taken with this tiny creature that seemed to want to figure me out. The others might have had new homes to go to, but Katherine was mine.

Where's that number? Here we go. Let this not be voice mail. Why am I so antsy about this? I guess I don't want to be too late. One ring....two....when people hint at disowning a pet, I'll do what I can to smooth the waters. "Hi, Beth, it's Diana...your phone message made me a little nervous, and I've been thinking about your kitty....Sure, and you've had such great cats in the past. Okay, so this new gal is an adult. Where'd she come from?....Animal Protective League, okay. Your message said she's urinating everywhere.....Aha, so not everywhere. ....Sure, it does matter. If she were peeing everywhere, she would surely need to see a vet, and as soon as possible. Lots of inappropriate behaviors have a medical basis. You always want to cover that possibility first. But when you say she's peeing right around the pan, it tells me she really wants to use that pan. Something is keeping her from climbing into it. Now the fun begins, because in Cat World we have the politics of the litter pan. Could be timing, meaning she's afraid to go into the pan when someone else has just used it or is lurking nearby. The litter may have a texture or a smell she doesn't like....Sure, and if she was a stray for a while, she had the advantage of using a clean location every time she eliminated. I know you keep the pans clean, so..... Oh, yeah, that does have a fairly aggressive fragrance. My first change would be a grain-based litter with no fragrance, then maybe another pan in a very quiet location....Does that give you enough to go on? Good. I think you have a plan. Vet visit, additional pan in a secluded location, and fragrance-free litter. Please stay in touch..... yes, she does have a lot to adjust to, and that doesn't worry me because I know how patient and kind you are. Oh, and try a calming agent, a plug-in or an additive for her water or moist food…. You have something?….Oh, good. She'll learn the ropes, her broken heart will mend, and the two of you will be best friends. Let me know how it goes……Sure, thanks, bye now."

I think she already knew all that. It's just that when you have a pet in the house acting inappropriately, you can easily become a little crazy and need someone to remind you of what to do. She called yesterday, and said she wasn't going to be available until this evening, and in the meantime she might return the kitty. She didn't and I know now she won't. Time, patience, and understanding. We owe the animals that.

All right, I managed by a few seconds to be off the phone by 9:00. Just one of my little rules. People can call my phone all hours of the day, and those calls are usually completely appropriate. My calls to them, however, have to fall within civilized limits.

Oh, check that. A huge moth under the center light. Let's watch our step. When the cats see it, we'll need to be out of the way. He won't have a problem here, but if he moves to the living room, where the table lamps are about two feet off the floor, he's done. Sammy, as you know, does not have a close relationship with gravity, and he can be nearly instantly airborne in order to catch a flying insect.

Let me take a few minutes to brush some unsuspecting victims here. If I sit down and stop moving, I'll just be too tired. Shadow and Sammy are my long-haired boys. "Hey, Shad-Man. Let's give you a little brushing. You know how disreputable you look after missing this for a few days." And now he's going to caterwaul. "There. Doesn't that feel good? How about that area under your chin? There's no way you can reach that. And your mane. Very pretty. You aren't complaining yet. What am I doing right? Feels good and you know it. Let's stand you up on your back feet so I can brush your chest. You are one big boy with lots of furry surface. See all that fur in the brush? You won't have to eat that. Great! All done."

Who's my next customer? "Katherine, really? Look at you walk right up to me. You enjoy this, don't you? You don't need much." I always look out for signs of fleas, especially this time of year. The last hurrah of the flea population in the fall always seems especially strong. Even one flea would be bad on any of my sweethearts, but as a pet sitter, the possibility is a nightmare.

"Maggie? Well, certainly, my dear. You'll need a bath in a few days, but let's keep the loose fur under control in the meantime. Okay, flop down. You are Miss Relaxation." It does my heart good when pets "ask" to be brushed. It shouldn't be torture. Some animals don't tolerate it well, and when we don't know their histories, it may be best to take it slow and easy. Silky and Herbie are both short-haired and intolerant, so we won't worry about them.

"Maggie, your skin and coat look so good." What a long time it took me to learn how to take care of this girl. When she was quite young she developed little red bumps that would turn into brown flaky spots. I imagined that the red bumps were sore, and that the flaky spots were itchy.

Maggie was always licking her bare tummy, where this stuff erupted the most. The vet believed it was a skin allergy and suggested that I wipe off her tummy with a wet cloth when she came in from outdoors, and to use fragrance-free laundry products. The groomer advised me to start giving her a good multivitamin. The woman at the health food store suggested flax seed oil. What do you think I did? Remember what my friend Frank told me. Get advice from the experts and then follow it. Yep, beautiful skin and coat.

"That should do it for you, gorgeous." And we're at about quarter after. I'm starting to feel it.

Hmm, who else, as long as I'm on a roll. Ah! The star-gazing lovers. Let's see if they're on the porch. "Cujo and Kiki, I thought you'd be here. Would you enjoy a little brushing?" Cujo jumps up and comes over whenever he sees a comb or brush. I do love those little combs with the rotating teeth for every coat type. "Oh, you sweet boy. Can you keep still? What are the chances? Poor to none, just 'cause you can't keep still when you get wound up. You're like your son. You love to have your throat and neck area brushed. Unlike you, he has quite a mane. Your purr is strong and steady. I'm not finding any loose fur in the brush. You're good as new, my love. Shall I brush your lady friend now?"

Kiki can't stand to be touched or picked up. She was nearly feral when I first knew her, and she's only somewhat better now. Somewhat surprisingly, she loves to be brushed. "Show us, Kiki, how much you love this." I have to move closer to her. The princess will not come to me. "Wanna smell it first? Sure, it smells like Cujo. Nice, huh? He is your man. Okay, I'm going to avoid your head and just brush your back and sides. Heads and tummies are personal. Do I have that right? That shy purr is starting up. Oh, sure, surprise me and flop over. I know better than to brush your tummy. I'll take that as a gesture, and not an invitation. Let's brush your sides a bit more and then we're done. I don't want to overdo it with you."

What an enviable romance those two have. On a starry night, they are always out here together, facing the same way, gazing into the darkness. I'm conflicted. I worry about their safety, and I am so much in awe of their relationship. Kiki will never be a good house cat, and Cujo won't be separated from her. If I could figure out an enclosure that would not be destroyed by wildlife, I would build it. The cats and I miss the screened porch that was so easily destroyed by the raccoons. Ah, well. What's life without dreams?

Maggie and I lured Cujo home from a house down the street. He used to sit at the front door there, yowling piteously. Clearly, he had been living there. The people, I'm guessing, got tired of his spraying or asking to be let out in the middle of the night. We encountered him as an adult, intact male. Oops. How does that keep happening? On our evening walks, I loaded my pockets with tiny pieces of boiled chicken, leaving a trail of them from Cujo's place to ours. He didn't exactly follow us home in that feel-good movie way. He seemed to ignore us, and I never saw him going for the bits of meat.

One night, an unearthly wailing made me sit straight up in bed. Assuming one of my cats was caught in something or in pain, I ran downstairs. I had no trouble finding my cats. They were all gathered, looking transfixed, at the cellar door. Once again, I was the last to figure it all out.

My cats knew what was going on. And Maggie – remember Maggie? – never bothered getting up. I quickly discovered that Cujo had broken out a basement window and let himself in. His vocalizing was apparently a request for permission to stay. He and my cats seemed to know each other already. As he climbed the steps, he was greeted by soft looks and question-mark tails. Only he and I needed to get acquainted. And, of course, we did.

And that crash just now is a lamp going over, so I know where Sammy and the moth are. "Excuse me, guys, let me get to the living room. I just have to see this." Sammy nails a moth in five seconds, and it looks as though we missed it. "Your favorite kind of treat, hey, Sammy? So fresh it's still twitching."

I'll let him enjoy that and we'll brush the boy. That will complete my meager efforts at grooming for today. "Come on, my golden boy. To the kitchen, and I think I hear the phone anyway."

"Hello?....Yes, Mary Ann...Right, I have you in the book for – let me see – I start next Monday....Oh, a liquid? That's easy enough. Yes, plenty of experience. ....Ooh, pretty long scratches, huh? ...With all the animals you've had, consider yourself lucky that this is the first kitty you've had to medicate....Well, I'm going by your place tomorrow, and I can stop and medicate her for you.....It would serve two purposes. I may be able to show you a way to make it less like a wrestling match, which by the way, the cat would usually win. And you didn't sound entirely confident that I knew how, so you can see for yourself. How does that sound? ....Oh, about 8:30.....Yes, I will charge you for the visit, but it will be worth it for all three of us...Good. See you then. Bye."

"Sammy, are you ready? Here we go, my love. And you above all I must watch for fleas. They like you too much, and that makes me wonder about your immune system. Let me look at you. You certainly seem healthy, full of spit and vinegar. Let's get the area around your neck. Feels nice, no? Sammy, I'm running out of steam and my back hurts. Let's give you a quick brush , especially that bushy tail. How did that moth taste? Good? Hold still. I'll bet the kill was more satisfying than the eating. I'm just guessing. Mostly dust with a little crunch, I'm assuming, maybe like an unsalted corn chip. Let's get the undercarriage. Quit squirming. Okay, Mr. Kitty, you're as fluffy as you're going to be. Love you, precious boy. You want me to hold you? Sure. Oh, I love your paws around my neck."

He thinks I'm his mother. He goes to sleep at night sucking on my nightgown.

"Yes, you are my special boy, now and always. My sweet monkey man. Down you go."

"Well, Maggie, let's look at the book. We had ten visits today and tomorrow we'll have, let's see, fifteen. A pretty solid day, with an early ending since Poppy's human will be home tomorrow afternoon. Great! We can watch a popcorn movie tomorrow night." That's a really cheesy movie we watch while throwing popcorn at the funniest parts. Of course, we eat our share and Maggie catches all of hers mid-air. She only misses a kernel if it's a bad throw on my part.

"Ready to go out? Go ahead." Maggie never goes beyond the illumination of the yard light. What a lucky girl she is. She's a pet sitter's dog, after all. She rides in the car every day, walks in all the best parks throughout Lorain County, and has play dates with only the classiest dogs. At the end of our work day, she has the comfy couch and popcorn.

"Good girl. Come on. Get your cookie. How about one of those turkey meatballs? What's in the fridge…. Oh, yes. Okay, sit. Good girl. Always a hit." Those things aren't bad. Got the recipe from one of those cookbooks for homemade dog food. I made half the batch for myself once with a splash of hot sauce and some salt and pepper. Very tasty.

CHAPTER 18

9:50 - End of Day

It's approaching 10:00, and if I didn't know it, Maggie would tell me. She decided long ago that this is our bedtime, and she won't climb the stairs without me. We have slept back to back since she was a puppy, and I don't know how either of us could sleep alone now.

"Ready for bed? Okay."

This beautiful life can't last. Nothing does, and so I treasure this time.

When I go out the door each day, I know there are pet sitters out there who are better at this than I am. Some have been professional groomers, breeders, obedience trainers, and vet techs. I have a background in none of those areas. I have lived with and have loved and admired animals since I was a child. So I bring that personal experience, as well as an interest in upholding high standards of responsibility and care. Additional knowledge comes from talking to other care providers and pet guardians, and doing lots of reading. The best teachers, as always, are the animals themselves. I have to hope that all pet sitters hold themselves to no lower a standard than mine.

When I started the business, I was penniless, hungry, and scared. Quite honestly, I just needed to make enough money to buy food and put gas in the car. I did it for myself and for my immediate needs, but I also knew it could be something more. I am still stunned and humbled when I stop to realize what a good life this work has given me.

Self-employment gives me the independence that suits my disposition so well. The nature of animal care requires that I keep learning and asking questions. That is one glorious feast for someone like me, because I always want to know more. I have little tolerance for petty workplace politics or pretentiousness, and the animals trouble me with neither.

The animals bring beauty, love, and the knowledge and skills for living fully – all to a degree that makes me humble in their presence. Well, I could go on, but I'd start repeating myself. My best friend is becoming restless now, her paw on that first step. As for me, I'm ready for a hot shower.

"Oh, Maggie, how much I love these days. Let's get some sleep now, sweet girl, so we can do it all again tomorrow."

About the Author

Diana Carter, dba The Petsitter, has been taking care of properly spoiled pets in Lorain County, Ohio since 1991.

Sources

Find a real pet sitter! Both of the following membership organizations provide locator services for pet sitting businesses through their websites. Just plug in your zip code.

National Association of Professional Pet Sitters (NAPPS)

Pet Sitters International (PSI)

Books mentioned in the text

Ackerley, J.R., *My Dog Tulip*

Benjamin, Carol Lea, *Second Hand Dog*

Beston, Henry, *The Outermost House*

Stroud, Robert, *Stroud's Digest on the Diseases of Birds*

Woodhouse, Barbara, *Dog Training My Way*

20528748R00122

Made in the USA
San Bernardino, CA
27 December 2018